Beginning Again

*Recovering your Innocence and Joy
through Confession*

Catherine de Hueck Doherty

*With reflections from the
Catechism of the Catholic Ch~*

MADONNA HOUSE PUBLICATIONS
Combermere, Ontario, Canada

Nihil Obstat:
Steven F. Ballard, J.C.L.
Censor Liborum, Nov. 3, 2004

Imprimatur:
✠ Richard W. Smith, S.T.D.
Bishop of Pembroke, Nov. 3, 2004

Madonna House Publications®
2888 Dafoe Rd, RR 2
Combermere ON K0J 1L0

www.madonnahouse.org/publications

Beginning Again by Catherine de Hueck Doherty (née Kolyschkine)

First Edition

Second printing, December 12, 2008 — Feast of Our Lady of Guadalupe

Compiled and edited by Martin Nagy
Research of Catherine Doherty's sources by Marian Heiberger
Design by Rob Huston (typeset in Berkeley Oldstyle and Balzano)

Excerpts from the English translation of the *Catechism of the Catholic Church*, 2d ed., for use in the United States of America copyright © 1994, 1997 United States Catholic Conference Inc.—Libreria Editrice Vaticana. Used with permission.

Unless otherwise noted, Scripture quotations are taken from the *New Jerusalem Bible*, copyright © 1985 Darton, Longman & Todd, London, and Doubleday, a division of Random House, Inc., New York.

Quotations from the Psalms are taken from *The Psalms*, copyright © 1966 Paulist Press, New York.

Library and Archives Canada Cataloguing in Publication Data

Doherty, Catherine de Hueck, 1896–1985.

  Beginning again : recovering your innocence and joy through confession / Catherine de Hueck Doherty.

Meditations, with extracts from the catechism of the Catholic Church.

ISBN 978-0-921440-94-9

  1. Confession—Catholic Church. I. Title.

BX2265.3.D64 2004   264'.020862   C2004-906200-X

Since God could create everything out of nothing, he can also, through the Holy Spirit, give spiritual life to sinners by creating a pure heart in them.

Catechism of the Catholic Church 298

"Behold, I make all things new."

Revelation 21:5 NAB

Healing

Conversion

Penance

Confession

Forgiveness

Reconciliation

Foreword

When you're in love, joy fills your heart. Your face glows. There's a song in the tone of your voice, an easy smile for those you meet, grace in your step. But what torture you feel after you've uttered an unguarded word or behaved callously toward your beloved! The distance feels like a chasm. You hear the echo in your heart. You're distracted and restless. You feel sick. Your sorrow torments you. You bathe your heart in tears. Can the innocence be recovered? The love rekindled? The joy restored?

Jesus is the Bridegroom, and we are his bride. Jesus knows our torment. He knows that we fear we've broken our relationship with him through sin. He knows our fear of being forgotten, rejected, abandoned. He knows our shame. But Jesus is the most generous of lovers. He established the sacrament of confession, so that we do not need to lose one moment of our life with him wallowing in guilt and misery.

Catherine Doherty tells us, "Christ's mercy was too immense to allow innocence to be destroyed without showing a way to restore it. So he gave us the sacraments of Penance and of the Eucharist which restore people to pristine innocence. It is yours for the asking, because he is in love with you." Only love could create such a generous gift for his beloved.

In the words of the *Catechism of the Catholic Church*, "the new birth of Baptism, the gift of the Holy Spirit, and the Body and Blood of Christ received as food have made us 'holy and without blemish,' just as the Church herself, the Bride of Christ, is 'holy and without blemish.'" However, this new life "can be weakened and even lost by sin." Therefore, the sacrament of Penance was established, because "the Lord Jesus Christ, physician of our souls and bodies, who forgave the sins of the paralytic and restored him to bodily health, has willed that his Church continue, in the power of the Holy Spirit, his work of healing and salvation, even among her own members."

As Catherine says, "Three cheers! You don't have to be perfect to be loved by God."

"When he celebrates the sacrament of Penance, the priest is fulfilling the ministry of the Good Shepherd who seeks the lost sheep, of the Good Samaritan who binds up wounds, of the Father who awaits the prodigal son and welcomes him on his return, and of the just and impartial judge whose judgment is both just and merciful. The priest is the sign and the instrument of God's merciful love for the sinner" (*Catechism*, 1465).

Through this earthen vessel—a priest, God the Father, Son, and Holy Spirit restores his child, his beloved to himself. The Byzantine Liturgy admirably expresses this mystery of forgiveness in one of the absolution prayers: "May the same God, who through the Prophet Nathan forgave David when he confessed his sins, who forgave Peter when he wept bitterly, the prostitute when she washed his feet with her tears, the publican, and the prodigal son, through me, a sinner, forgive you both in this life and in the next and enable you to appear before his awe-inspiring tribunal without condemnation, he who is blessed for ever and ever. Amen" (*Catechism*, 1481).

Catherine reminds us, "Stainless must be our wedding garment when we come before the gaze of the Bridegroom. We can keep it white and pure from baptism to death, for his grace is always there to help us. But we are weak, weighed down with the flesh, the world, and the devil. We fall and stain our baptismal robes. Oh, the goodness of God! They can be washed clean, and for this he offers us the confessional, where, in utter abandonment of love, he washes them with his own Precious Blood."

No matter what you've done, you can embrace Jesus and Jesus will embrace you. No sin, no accusation can stand between Jesus and you. And you can forgive yourself. The sacrament of Reconciliation washes you, purifies you, makes you fresh, makes you new through the grace of the Holy Spirit, through the Blood of Jesus, through the prayer and ministry of the Church when the priest blesses you and prays, "God, the Father of mercies, through the death and the resurrection of his Son has reconciled the world to himself and sent the Holy Spirit among us for the forgiveness of sins; through the ministry of the Church may God give you pardon and peace, and I absolve you from your sins in the name of the Father, and of the Son, and of the Holy Spirit."

What joy! You're clean. You're free, again. You can gaze into the eyes of Jesus with love and gratitude, your innocence restored. You can begin again. You can fall in love with Jesus all over again. You can live the joy that he has always wanted for you.

Catherine's book isn't meant to be an extensive curriculum on confession. Rather, Catherine speaks from her heart as a laywoman, one called to constantly give formation to the community God led her to found, as well as to the wider Church through her lectures and writings and the witness of her life. Let Catherine in her tender, passionate recounting of moments from her own love life with God teach you how to return to your Beloved's heart through the sacrament of confession after you've been distracted and forgotten him who loves you more than you love yourself.

Martin Nagy, Editor
Feast of the Queenship of Mary, 2004

It may help the reader to know that the teachings and meditations on confession by Catherine were selected from her diaries, spiritual readings, lectures, and writings from the 1930's to the 1980's. They represent the development of her thinking over a period of about 50 years, from her thirties to her eighties.

Chapter I

Healing

O purify me, then I shall be clean;
O wash me, I shall be whiter than snow.
A pure heart create for me, O God,
put a steadfast spirit within me.

Psalm 50:9,12

The Physician of Our Souls

The Lord Jesus Christ, physician of our souls and bodies, who forgave the sins of the paralytic and restored him to bodily health, has willed that his Church continue, in the power of the Holy Spirit, his work of healing and salvation, even among her own members. This is the purpose of the two sacraments of healing: the sacrament of Penance and the sacrament of Anointing of the Sick (Catechism of the Catholic Church, 1421).

Jesus Christ instituted this beautiful sacrament. He said so clearly to the apostles, "I give you the keys of the kingdom of heaven: whatever you bind on earth shall be considered bound in heaven; whatever you loose on earth shall be considered loosed in heaven" (Mt 16:19); "Receive the Holy Spirit, for those whose sins you forgive, they are forgiven; for those whose sins you retain, they are retained" (Jn 20:22–23).

It is a terrible, awesome power that those men have, the successors of the apostles. One of our children, a very ordinary man with humble hands of clay, has a power beyond our under-standing, the power to loose and the power to bind. The mystery of the priesthood is immense.

But bending our knees and going to confession is one of our great difficulties. We do not want to go. Why don't we go to confession?

If we have sinned, we have to walk into the confessional and say clearly and simply, "Father, I have sinned. Here are my sins. Absolve me, please."

And a man, an ordinary man, fat or thin, with teeth or without teeth, says, "I absolve you."

What happens? A miracle happens.

God said, "Which of these is easier to say, 'Your sins are forgiven' or 'Get up, pick up your bed and walk'" (Mk 2:9), thereby making those proud people understand that he had powers beyond all other powers. He had the power to forgive sin.

In that confessional, a voice in many accents, but the same voice of Jesus Christ says, "Take up your bed and walk," meaning your sins are forgiven. That is what the priest says.

Well, that is joy, isn't it? When I was training in psychiatry, we had a professor who was an atheist, but respected every religion. When he lectured, he used to say to the nurses, "The greatest therapy in the world is the Roman Catholic confession." You walk out of that confession with a joy transforming you from your head to your feet, "I have been forgiven!"

Obviously, we are sinners. God knows that, and he consorted with sinners, so he has given us a sacrament that I call "the kiss of Christ." It is Christ's kiss of peace, of forgiveness. The Russians call confession "the kiss of Christ," because it says in the Song of Songs, "Let him kiss me with the kisses of his mouth" (Sg 1:2).

That is what Christ does when we kneel down and confess seemingly to a human being. And our faith is like fresh air. We accept it. We breathe it. We are on our knees. We believe, "*Credo*. I believe. I believe that this man is divinely appointed to forgive sins." When he speaks, God speaks. And a joy beyond all joys fills the heart of the person.

Today it is a sacrament that people don't want to go to on Saturday or Sunday or whatever day it is. Foolish! Childish!

So you don't want to be kissed by Christ? You don't want to kneel down and say to a man, "I have sinned," and to believe that sitting there in a chair, inside or outside the confessional—it doesn't make much difference—sits Christ, and it is he who says, "I forgive you." It is all about Christ himself. He says, "I absolve you."

I look at priests—this funny chap, who is the priest—fat, thin, tall, short—and in faith, I see a beautiful sight. I see Christ taking me in his arms and consoling me while I weep at his feet in the confessional.

We have a dislike lately, of confession. There are all kinds of confessions going on, like communal, general absolution. The Church sometimes allows general confession. "In case of grave necessity recourse may be had to a communal celebration of reconciliation with general confession and general absolution. Grave necessity of this sort can arise when there is imminent danger of death....Grave necessity can also exist when...there are not enough confessors...so that the penitents...would be deprived of sacramental grace or Holy Communion for a long time" (*Catechism*, 1483).

For instance, during the war when there was no time to form a line before a single chaplain, the Church gave absolution to thousands of people, who, of course, had in their heart a great sorrow and repentance. I myself have been through two revolutions and two wars, and experienced that sort of situation, but in ordinary life we need to talk to Jesus Christ in personal confession about things that we want to hide from other people, and then to get absolved of them. The voice that is talking to you in confession is Christ's voice, provided you have faith in what a priest is.

"Individual, integral confession and absolution remain the only ordinary way for the faithful to reconcile themselves with God and the Church unless physical or moral impossibility excuses from this kind of confession. There are profound reasons for this. Christ…personally addresses every sinner: 'My son, your sins are forgiven.' He is the physician tending each one of the sick who need him to cure them. He raises them up and reintegrates them into fraternal communion. Personal confession is thus the form most expressive of reconciliation with God and with the Church" (*Catechism*, 1484).

There is this man to whom I can go and tell anything and everything. I can really tell the priest what is in my heart and the guilt that eats at me or whatever, knowing that he is not going to break what they call the "seal" of the confessional. "Given the delicacy and greatness of this ministry and the respect due to persons, the Church declares that every priest who hears confessions is bound under very severe penalties to keep absolute secrecy regarding the sins that his penitents have confessed to him. He can make no use of knowledge that confession gives him about penitents' lives. This secret, which admits of no exceptions, is called the 'sacramental seal,' because what the penitent has made known to the priest remains 'sealed' by the sacrament" (*Catechism*, 1467).

As a result, the Roman Catholic clergy, to their tremendous honor and heroism, have never revealed the secret of the confessional. They have been tortured, they have had terrible things done to them, but they haven't opened their mouths. It's rather consoling, isn't it?

What is more, the priest says, "I absolve you," and something happens. Suddenly in a very ordinary priest, you feel the immensity of God.

Christ gave the priest a special power so that, when he utters a few words of absolution, Christ washes our soul and embraces us in love and reconciliation. Christ comes to us, therefore, in such tremendous simplicity of love that our breath should be taken away. He comes to us in the guise of a priest.

So then, approach a priest with the understanding that he has God in him in a special manner through his ordination. Approach him as you would approach Christ.

You might say, "What of the priest who is sinful and unholy?" You ask this because you haven't been given the full knowledge of what priesthood really is. Therefore, you don't realize that the seal of priesthood has been etched in the soul of this poor, sinful man. It has been placed there by the fire of the Holy Spirit and the touch of the Father's hand, and he can never lose that gift.

Confession is such a wonderful thing that everybody should be rushing there. I love confession. Absolution falls on your ears like oil on your wounds. The forgiveness of God envelops you like a mantle. The confessional is the altar of mercy.

Only love could devise such a thing. At any hour, our souls can be washed clean and whiter than snow in the most holy sacrament of Penance. We can become little children again, newly baptized. As I come out of the confessional, a little baby and I are equal.

Think of it, dearly beloved. Think of what this most holy sacrament of confession means. Spendthrift of love, our Lord, gives it to us to bathe our souls and make them alive again, resurrecting them from sin in a mercy that knows no end until we die.

What does he do when you go to confession to himself in the priest? His precious blood flows again and washes you clean. It is as if you were standing, again, somewhere during his Passion where his blood flowed and one drop fell on you. One drop of his blood can wash the world clean.

Christ Absolves You

Since it is ultimately Christ who acts and effects salvation through the ordained minister, the unworthiness of the latter does not prevent Christ from acting (Catechism of the Catholic Church, 1584).

Ordination is something mysterious and beautiful. A young man walks up three steps, the bishop puts his hands on his head, and the Holy Spirit descends into him. If you have faith, you can see now that Christ enters into that person. You go to the confessional and the priest says, "I absolve you," but it's Christ who is speaking to you, Christ is absolving you.

The feeling that I have really forgotten God, that I have let him down, saddens us to such a point, or should, that we can't bear it any more. Now what do you or I do? You lay the burden of that tiredness, of that forgetfulness, into the hands of a man who is bound never to talk about it and who represents Christ. The gentle sacrament of confession, brings you there.

In this part of the world, you appraise the priest with your brain. You see a drunken guy staggering at night through a village or your parish; or you know that Father is an alcoholic and not in Alcoholics Anonymous, yet. You know a lot of things about the priest. Since you don't approve of who he is, you say to yourself, "Me, go to confession to this guy? Never!" That's because you don't know much about the tenderness of Christ, about what a priest is, about so many things that you should know about.

When the Revolution came to Russia, we were forbidden to go to churches and forbidden to perform ceremonies. So the Catholic priest would announce that we were going to have a Mass at three or four o'clock in the morning. People would walk in the shadow of the houses and sneak in. Nothing but little tapers were lit by the Blessed Sacrament, and the Mass was very short.

One day, the door was flung open by Red soldiers just as the priest had consecrated the host and was slowly bringing it down. One shot and the priest was dead, and the Blessed Sacrament rolled on the floor.

The Red soldiers walked in, marched to the Blessed Sacrament, squashed it with their heels, turned to us and said, "Where is your God? Under our heels."

Then, an old man said (I can still hear his reedy voice), "Father, forgive them, even if they know what they do." With that, they departed.

Little bits of the host were still there. The old man gathered them reverently and gave us communion. That was the last communion I had in Petrograd.

We lived under a constant death sentence. Put yourself in that position. If there was only one priest in Petrograd, I would crawl on my belly, even if I knew he had fornicated, committed adultery, was a drunkard, had stolen, had murdered—name the sins—I would crawl on my belly to him. Why? Because he is Christ. He can absolve my sins even while he wallows in his. He can give me the pure Body of Christ, while his hands are dirty.

That is the tenderness of Christ to us. That is his love for us. That is why a priest is a priest to us, or should be. I would be idiotic to appraise a priest by the standards of my puny little mind.

"St. Augustine states this forcefully:

"'As for the proud minister, he is to be ranked with the devil. Christ's gift is not thereby profaned: what flows through him keeps its purity, and what passes through him remains clear and reaches the fertile earth.…The spiritual power of the sacrament is indeed comparable to light: those to be enlightened receive it in its purity, and if it should pass through defiled beings, it is not itself defiled'" (*Catechism*, 1584).

Remember, Christ chose twelve. One sold him down the river. Another denied him. Where were the others when he was arrested? They fled, and you couldn't see them for the dust at their heels. But those are the ones he chose to give us the sacraments.

I often listen to the voice of priests who absolve. Some are bored, and some indifferent, and some are happy and rejoice with me. I'm sure that Christ wants them to put a little pep into it, even if they spend two or three or four hours in the confessional, or fifteen hours as did St. John Vianney, the Curé of Ars. He put pep into it. That's how he got canonized. So, a little pep would go a long way. But it doesn't matter, because after all, they don't absolve me, Christ does.

When you say to a man, "I have sinned," you have to believe that this chap called a "priest," whatever he might be, is Christ, and it is Christ who says, "I forgive you. I absolve you." Get that straight. This must always be there before you in the infinite totality of faith. It isn't the priest who is absolving in confession, it's Christ.

The Kiss of Christ

"Through the Holy Spirit we are restored to paradise, led back to the Kingdom of heaven, and adopted as children, given confidence to call God 'Father' and to share in Christ's grace, called children of light and given a share in eternal glory." (St. Basil, Catechism of the Catholic Church, *736)*

When I was a young girl, my mother said, "Catherine, it's time for you to go to confession and be kissed by Christ." Isn't that a nice introduction for a child? So I would go to church, kneel before a priest, and tell him my thoughts.

But in my imagination it was much more than that. My mother very gently and simply explained it. I had committed a fault and knew that God wouldn't like it, so I sort of ran towards him and, sitting on his lap and putting my arms around his neck, I would kiss him—like I did my father—and tell him how sorry I was for having done something he didn't like.

In my imagination, Christ hugged me and said something like, "That's all right, little girl. I know it's not easy to always do the right thing."

Then, he would kiss me and bless me and say, "Now go and play."

I realized that when you grow up, you receive another kiss. You sin and say, "I'm sorry." Slowly, a strange face that nobody knows and yet everybody knows bends down and touches mine, and I experience the words, "Let him kiss me with the kisses of his mouth."

This is what confession is. In a sense, his lips touch yours, and fire and flame enter your heart and cleanse the sin.

It's a simple thing, not very complicated. Perhaps the way my mother taught me stayed with me. I was never afraid to go. Always, before my eyes, were the love and forgiveness of God and his immense mercy.

Many people have rejected confession. They are not interested. They don't go there very much. What they miss! They miss being kissed by God. I always feel a little sad when people don't go to confession often, because they miss so much. Above all, they miss a kiss from Christ.

Unfortunately, we are all sinners. But God loved to be with sinners. That's a consolation. Let us simply, in a childlike way, allow our hearts to kneel (hearts kneel, you know) and ask forgiveness of God. For God said, unless you are a child, you don't go into heaven (Mk 10:15). Then, we ask forgiveness of everybody we've hurt, even if they are not here. Even if they're dead. Simply say, "Please, forgive me."

Didn't Christ say, "I have come not for those who are healthy, but for the sick, and not for the just, but for sinners" (Lk 5:31–32)? He spoke of himself as a physician, a healer. So what is all this talk about confession? Who of us would not mind standing in line before a doctor's office if he or she were sick? Do we really mind standing in line to be kissed by Christ?

For those of us who have been guided by our parents, it seems rather incomprehensible that so much fuss should be raised about going to confession. A sick person goes to a doctor; so a childlike soul goes to Christ to be consoled, to be healed, to be forgiven. It is like a lover running into the arms of the Beloved.

If any one of you is away from the sacraments, this is the moment to reconsider. The Father is waiting for you. Why not run to him and say, "I'm sorry."

Love Restores Your Innocence

Because we are dead or at least wounded through sin, the first effect of the gift of love is the forgiveness of our sins. The communion of the Holy Spirit in the Church restores to the baptized the divine likeness lost through sin (Catechism of the Catholic Church, 734).

There is a great miracle in God, a great gift of God—lost innocence can be restored.

Have we told others about this gift? Have we spoken to our friends, to our enemies, to ourselves about it—we who are supposedly bringing the Good News to the world?

Confession is the way to restore innocence. Once we have repented and have met Christ in this sacrament, he touches us in our inmost being, and we become as innocent as newborn babies.

Even though God can restore innocence through this sacrament, we go around very sophisticatedly and say to others, "Oh, you go to confession? You know, that is passé; it just isn't done anymore." I've heard that over and over again. It's another way of taking away from the innocent the return to their innocence. Have we got the right to do this?

Christ's mercy was too immense to allow innocence to be destroyed without showing a way to restore it. So he gave us the sacraments of Penance and of the Eucharist which restore people to pristine innocence.

It is yours for the asking, because he is in love with you. How utterly loving God is!

Let us be watchful that we are not guilty of tearing off innocence from anybody. It's a mantle that you can tear off. And if it happens that we do, let us weave a mantle out of our compunction, out of our sorrow, out of our repentance, and put it on that person by leading them to the one place where innocence can be restored, the lips of our Lord Jesus Christ.

Beginning Again

Since God could create everything out of nothing, he can also, through the Holy Spirit, give spiritual life to sinners by creating a pure heart in them. (Catechism of the Catholic Church, 298).

With God, every moment is the moment of beginning again.

This means that anyone in Christ who is repentant and reconciled is new. Shiny new, like a newly baptized child.

That is one reason why I implore you constantly and implore God for you constantly that you get rid of your guilt complexes. How can you have a guilt complex about something that has been confessed, opened up, revealed to God, about something that has been wiped off by him who gives you this shining moment?

Every moment is the moment of renewal, if we have forgiveness, repentance, reconciliation. It is so beautiful. It makes you pick yourself up and say, "My God, this is who I am, and this is who my brothers and sisters are."

How wonderful it is to wake up in the morning and to have as a first thought, "God loves me"! How healing to let that beautiful thought be absorbed through our spiritual pores, as a sponge absorbs water! Yes, God loves me. We are saved sinners. We know that we will probably continue to sin in one way or another, but sinner or saint, God loves me.

Our sins that are past, why even remember them? God has forgotten them. Why is it that we want to remember them? A forgiven sin does not exist in the mind of God. God is not a stingy forgiver who remembers our sins for the rest of our lives. The mercy of God is infinite. Faith permits us to know the mercy of God. It enables us to read and absorb what God said in torment while he was dying: "Today you will be with me in paradise" (Lk 23:43).

In our houses, there are showers and baths and basins to wash in, and soap to wash with. But we forget that as we wake up in the morning, there is a whole sea of God's mercy, warm and pleasant, waiting for us to plunge into, so that we can be cleansed for the day ahead. God's mercy takes away *every* kind of stain.

There will be times when we will have to go to confession, which is a way that this sea of mercy washes over us. But we should wake up each morning, knowing that God loves us, that he died for us, that he is in our midst.

We will have good days and bad days, peaceful days and unpeaceful ones. But the majority of them will be peaceful, if we remember that God loves us. His love binds us together. He wants us to be childlike. I think he desires that we should hold hands and dance sometime during the day, at least in our hearts, so that the joy of his heart may enter into ours.

He is open. What is more open than a naked man, pierced with nails, hanging high on a cross? Naked he came out of his mother's womb; naked he died. Nakedness is revelation. In his case, it is the revelation of love. This shows us the beautiful face of hope. Fear can have no place, for perfect love banishes away fear (1 Jn 4:18).

This is the time, dearly beloved, to understand how much you are beloved by God. You are lovable. Never mind how you feel about yourself. You are beloved by God deeply, profoundly, totally.

Having understood this, we feel his fingers covered with clay and spittle, touching the eyes of our hearts and revealing to us that we are able to love one another. We can really, deeply, beautifully, love one another. We can accept peacefully all of the little difficulties with one another (present in any family), for nothing matters very much as long as we love one another.

We should devote this to prayer, so that we will absorb into our deepest heart the fact that we are beloved by God. And we will gain that immense grace—charism—to love one another as the gospel calls us to do. Why not start now? Why not let go of all the inhibitions; the anger toward oneself, and toward another; the feeling of self-pity and loneliness? Throw them all out, and allow our tired souls and tired hearts to expand.

Hold hands. Be childlike. Love one another. Let us sing an alleluia in our hearts.

Christ is in our midst and loves us with a tremendous passion. The Lord desires a new order for those coming to new life in his body. His desire for change in our lives far exceeds our own. The Lord desires for each of us to have a new heart, a heart committed to him, a realization of being loved and valued by him, and a spirit of loving service to our brothers and sisters.

Creation is the making of something from nothing, a new creation. A new creation is the most radical and total type of change that man could conceive. God wants to heal us, change us, make a new creation of each of us.

The mercy of God tenderly, sweetly, delicately, mercifully, compassionately, envelops me. Yet, his mercy is, also, always overpowering. It seems to shake me to the very bottom of my being, so that I want to continually cry out, "Glory! Glory! Alleluia. I love you, Lord. I thank you, Lord. I thank you for taking me out of whatever I was."

O Lord of Hosts,
I stand before you
with a heart full of tears
and a soul filled with repentance
for all the moments I have been away from you.
Sins of my past life stand before me
in all their horrible nakedness.
And I have only your mercy to fall back upon.
But, then, it is an infinite mercy,
so I throw myself into its sea
and swim to the shore of your love.
Amen.

Chapter Two

Conversion

*I shall cleanse you of all your defilement
and all your idols.
I shall give you a new heart,
and put a new spirit in you....
I shall put my spirit in you....
You shall be my people
And I will be your God.*

Ezekiel 36:25–28

Return to the Father

*Conversion is first of all a work of the grace of God
who makes our hearts return to him: "Restore us to
thyself, O Lord, that we may be restored!" (Lam
5:21). God gives us the strength to begin anew*
(Catechism of the Catholic Church, 1432).

Recently, I reread the story of the prodigal son
(Lk 15:11–32). I often read it. It is one of my
favorite parables. And I said to myself, "Now
think about it, Catherine. Think about it with

your heart, not with your head." It is the heart that understands. The head understands a little, but the heart understands much more.

"The process of conversion and repentance was described by Jesus in the parable of the prodigal son, the center of which is the merciful father....Only the heart of Christ who knows the depths of his Father's love could reveal to us the abyss of his mercy in so simple and beautiful a way" (*Catechism*, 1439).

There was a father, and he had two sons. One son wanted his inheritance, immediately. He wanted everything, *now*. Not tomorrow, not yesterday—now.

The father, being a father, knows very well what is going to happen to the one who claims his inheritance. He has been around long enough. But he gives it to him.

And so it happens that the son turns to wine, women, and song—riotous living.

Finally, he is reduced to looking after swine. Nobody seems to give him much to eat, so he eats the husks and food given to the swine.

Then, he has a brilliant idea. The son thinks, "It would be so much better to go and be a servant in my father's house, because at least they will feed me."

And so the son goes—*every day* of a man's life is the acceptable time for beginning again. We need to begin again—now—today—for it is not only the "acceptable time," it is the *urgent* time (2 Cor 6:2).

What happens to the father?

I read in between the lines, sometimes. I have a vivid imagination, so don't think that what I saw is exactly how it is said in the gospel. But reading it over and over again, I can just see the father periodically going outside and looking, straining his eyes, just hoping that there beyond the horizon, his son will come.

One day, as he was looking, lo and behold, there in the distance, he saw a speck. But he knew who it was. He recognized him, as only fathers and mothers can do.

He immediately called a servant. First, he ran towards the approaching silhouette. But as he ran he must have asked the servant to bring a ring and lovely cloak.

The father and son meet.

The son falls on his knees and begs pardon of his father. But before the words are out of his mouth, the father picks him up, presses him to his heart, and, in a spirit of tremendous joy, puts the ring on his finger and covers his rags with this beautiful cloak.

"The fascination of illusory freedom, the abandonment of the father's house; the extreme misery in which the son finds himself after squandering his fortune; his deep humiliation at finding himself obliged to feed swine, and still worse, at wanting to feed on the husks the pigs ate; his reflection on all he has lost; his repentance and decision to declare himself guilty before his father; the journey back; the father's generous welcome; the father's joy—all these are characteristics of the process of conversion. The beautiful robe, the ring, and the festive banquet are symbols of that new life—pure, worthy, and joyful—of anyone who returns to God and to the bosom of his family, which is the Church" (*Catechism*, 1439).

After confession, I sometimes feel like a tired traveler who at last has put his load down.

We need to be reminded often of the goodness of God and his mercy, so that when the day is ended, we may come to him without fears, with hearts truly filled with sorrow for our sins of omission and commission. We, also, need to pray to have a humble and contrite heart. Contrition is essential. A good confession is started with an examination of conscience, continued with deep sorrow and contrition and a resolution not to sin any more with the help of God's grace.

God loves me. He loves me when I am good and when I am not so good, because he loves sinners. He forgives them, too. God's mercy is infinite and so are his love, his goodness, and his forgiveness. What a consoling thought this is. It's hard to imagine such goodness—but all God's attributes are hard to imagine. The fruit of confession is forgiveness from God and his utter forgetfulness of your sin.

This is what God does to us, over and over and over again. The Lord, like the father, puts a ring upon my finger. It is a seal upon my heart of his forgiveness.

Respond to Jesus' Touch

The human heart is converted by looking upon him whom our sins have pierced (Catechism of the Catholic Church, 1432).

Paul was a major sinner. He tried to destroy the Christians. He said:

"As for me, I once thought it was my duty to use every means to oppose the name of Jesus.... I myself threw many of the saints into prison... and when they were sentenced to death, I cast my vote against them." (Acts 26:9–10).

Suddenly, the inexhaustible mercy and forgiveness of God touched him, and he fell off his horse.

"I was going to Damascus...and at midday...I saw a light brighter than the sun come down from heaven....We all fell to the ground, and I heard a voice saying to me...'Why are you persecuting me? It is hard for you, kicking like this against the goad.'

"Then I said: 'Who are you, Lord?'

"And the Lord answered, 'I am Jesus, and you are persecuting me. But get up and stand on your feet, for I have appeared to you for this reason: to appoint you as my servant and as witness of this vision in which you have seen me, and of others in which I shall appear to you. I shall deliver you from the people...to whom I am sending you to open their eyes, so that they may turn from darkness to light, from the dominion of Satan to God, and receive, through faith in me, forgiveness of their sins and a share in the inheritance of the sanctified'" (Acts 9:1–19; 22:5–16; 26:1–18).

He was blind for a little while, but he received the gift of faith, and he passed it on.

Yet, Paul acknowledged himself to be a sinner. This is beautiful.

"I thank Christ Jesus our Lord who has given me strength and who judged me faithful enough to call me into his service, even though I used to be a blasphemer and did all I could to injure and discredit the faith" (1 Tm 1:12–13).

But Paul had no guilt complex.

"Mercy, however, was shown me, because until I became a believer I had been acting in ignorance and the grace of our Lord filled me with faith and with the love that is in Jesus Christ" (1 Tm 1:13–14).

Paul was absolutely sure that he was going to get this crown of righteousness.

"Here is a saying that you can rely on and nobody should doubt: that Christ Jesus came into this world to save sinners. I myself am the greatest of them. And if mercy has been shown to me, it is because Jesus Christ meant to make me the greatest evidence of his inexhaustible patience for all the other people who would later have to trust in him to come to eternal life" (1 Tm 1:15–16).

Paul knew the merciful God.

Jesus Does Not Condemn You

During his public life Jesus not only forgave sins, but also made plain the effect of this forgiveness: he reintegrated forgiven sinners into the community of the People of God from which sin had alienated or even excluded them (Catechism of the Catholic Church, 1443).

There is the story of the woman caught in adultery. The scribes and Pharisees found this woman in adultery, and they brought her before Christ "making her stand in full view of everybody" (Jn 8:3).

What does Christ do?

He wasn't even curious. He evidently turned his back and was writing something in the sand.

"As they persisted with their question, he looked up," and, quietly, from the back, he said, "'If there is one of you who has not sinned, let him be the first to throw a stone at her" (Jn 8:7).

"Then he bent down," and he went on writing (Jn 8:8). Look at the delicacy. He turned his back to that woman. She was ashamed to be before this prophet, and so delicately he turned his back, because he is a lover of men.

After awhile he said, "Woman, did anybody condemn you, throw the stones?"

There was no one to throw stones, because the Jews had sense enough to disappear. There wasn't one of them without a sin.

Some people are afraid of the judgment of God. Next to Christ on the cross is a thief. Christ says to him, "Today you shall be with me in paradise" (Lk 23:43). That's the judgment of Christ. God sent his Son, and we say, "God is love."

Now how does Love judge? First, delicacy—turning around and not looking, and writing something in the sand. Then, Christ said to her peacefully—you can feel the gentleness and goodness of his voice, "Neither do I condemn you" (Jn 8:11). "Go in peace, and sin no more."

God Forgets Your Sin

This endeavor of conversion is not just a human work. It is the movement of a "contrite heart," drawn and moved by grace to respond to the merciful love of God who loved us first (Catechism of the Catholic Church, 1428).

We are riddled with guilt. One of the things everyone is worried about is God's justice. People shake and say, "Oh, I am a louse, I am a sinner." Of course you are a sinner. But never forget you are a *saved* sinner.

Why is everyone going around wallowing in his or her past sins? After we go to confession, we say, "Oh, I don't feel that I am cleansed." "But if we acknowledge our sins, then God who is faithful and just will forgive our sins and cleanse us from everything that is wrong" (1 Jn 1:9). When you really repent, you are as clean as a little newborn baby. What's the score? "As far as the east is from the west so far does he remove our sins" (Ps 102:12). Why should I worry about what happened to me or the last mortal sin that I committed? God has forgotten it, so why should I remember? "He says…'I will forgive their iniquities and never call their sins to mind'" (Heb 8:12; 10:17).

When we continue to feel guilty, there is something behind it—there is lack of trust in

God. Oh yes, we know that God forgives sinners. We believe it, so we say. But do we? Where is our confidence in God, our love of God, our trust in God, our faith, and our hope? Where are they? If they were there we would not be racked with guilt.

The East very seldom feels guilty, because, you see, they rely on the mercy of God very strongly, and they go to confession. The only time that I feel guilty is the time between the committing of the sin and going to confession. But when I'm absolved, I forget that I ever sinned. Why should I remember if God doesn't? Think about it.

God is merciful to repentant sinners. Yet, in our society there is this terrible emotional problem of guilt. You can tell people again and again that God forgives, but they refuse to believe it. In the first place, they refuse to believe that he loves them. And they refuse to believe that he loves them, because they don't forgive themselves. They say, "If I cannot forgive myself, how can God?" Again, our little brains want to reduce God to our own stature. It is a tragic situation, because if only we accepted this premise that God forgives us, we would be a laughing, joyous, guiltless, happy generation.

Consider the ways of God with men. To begin with, God loved us first. Now, try to absorb this.

Absorb it. Take it into your skin, into your pores, into everything. God loved us first.

Well, we are not very lovable, but somehow or other he managed it. He loved us first. The picture of Christ is one of such gentleness. He looks at us, and he loves us so much. He wants to take us and press us to his heart. But we say, "No, no!" We don't want to hear this stuff. Still he loves us. He continues to love us to the very end.

Why don't we approach God with the utter simplicity of children? Suppose we lived in Nazareth when he lived there. He would have attracted us by his personality. I am sure a lot of young people and old people talked to him. He was wise. And they were peaceful about it and happy. But we are forever searching our hearts with our little brains, that's our problem.

God's way with man is so gentle, so gentle. He was accused of hobnobbing with prostitutes and tax collectors, and he did. When he was speaking, to whom was he talking? Mostly to cooks and waiters—ordinary people. The big shots were at the back, writing down something on their tablets to condemn him with. Very few of them came to him. The poor, the humble, the unimportant, they came. And that's the kind of people we all are. God deals with all of us with great gentleness and always with great kindness. It's *we* who attribute to him great severity, the big stick, and so forth.

Why do we go around thinking that we are the lousiest people on earth, with a self-image almost of despair? Why attribute that sort of lousy self-image to oneself, when I have been created by God; I am an icon of God; he died to save me. I am lovable, and so I cannot have a lousy image of myself unless I have a lousy image of God.

To us are addressed the words in Isaiah, "It is I, I, who wipe out, for my own sake, your offenses; your sins I remember no more" (Is 43:25 NAB). "No need to recall the past. No need to think about what was done before" (Is 43:18). On reading that, can anyone have a feeling of guilt left?

How can a Christian feel guilty once he has read the gospel? A thief asked Jesus, "Jesus, remember me when you come into your kingdom." Jesus replied, "Indeed, I promise you, today you will be with me in paradise" (Lk 23:39–43).

This word of a man on a cross, dying for love of humanity is a consolation for all who feel guilty because of sins. Let guilt be wiped out. "Today you will be with me in paradise." If anyone of you feels guilty and you know that you deserve it, fear not. Look at Jesus Christ. If you say, "Have mercy on me," and look with eyes of faith, you will see an unseen hand wipe out all your sins and misdemeanors. You will realize that you are already in paradise, because he who is merciful dwells in you, and where he is, there is paradise. It is as simple as that.

Who can feel guilty when the hand of mercy holds him? If I repent, I simply say, "Sorry, Lord," and he has already forgiven. Place yourself before Jesus Christ, and slowly, fear will leave, and guilt will leave, and we will have left a sinner who has started to love. Look at the prodigal. Think about it. Cheer up. There is nothing to worry about.

Do You Love Me

Jesus' look of infinite mercy drew tears of repentance from Peter and, after the Lord's resurrection, a three-fold affirmation of love for him (Catechism of the Catholic Church, 1429).

"At that instant, while he was still speaking, the cock crowed, and the Lord turned and looked straight at Peter, and Peter remembered what the Lord had said to him, 'Before the cock crows today, you will have disowned me three times.' And he went outside and wept bitterly" (Lk 22:55–62).

What must Peter have felt when Christ appeared to him after his resurrection and said, "Peter, do you love me?" three times? "When they had finished breakfast, Jesus said to Simon

Peter, 'Simon, son of John, do you love me more than these?...He then said to him a second time, "Simon, son of John, do you love me?"...He said to him the third time, "Simon, son of John, do you love me?" (Jn 21:15–17).

Christ never spoke of Peter's betrayal. Peter went around talking about it everywhere, but Christ never mentioned it. Peter must have felt liberated from the terrible sin of betrayal.

You Bring Joy to Heaven

Jesus invites sinners to the table of the kingdom: "I came not to call the righteous, but sinners." He invites them to that conversion without which one cannot enter the kingdom, but shows them in word and deed his Father's boundless mercy for them and the vast "joy in heaven over one sinner who repents" (Catechism of the Catholic Church, 545).

There are the parables of the lost drachma and the lost sheep.

"The tax collectors and sinners, meanwhile, were all seeking his company to hear what he had to say, and the Pharisees and scribes complained. 'This man,' they said, 'welcomes sinners and eats with them.' So he spoke this parable to them.

"'What man among you with a hundred sheep, losing one, would not leave the ninety-nine in the wilderness and go after the missing one till he found it? And when he found it, would he not joyfully take it on his shoulders and then, when he got home, call together his friends and neighbors? "Rejoice with me," he would say, "I have found my sheep that was lost."

"'In the same way, I tell you, there will be more rejoicing in heaven over one repentant sinner than over ninety-nine virtuous men who have no need of repentance.

"'Or, again, what woman with ten drachmas would not, if she lost one, light a lamp and sweep out the house and search thoroughly till she found it? And then, when she had found it, call together her friends and neighbors? "Rejoice with me," she would say, "I have found the drachma I lost."

"'In the same way, I tell you, there is rejoicing among the angels of God over one repentant sinner'" (Lk 15:1–10).

The lost drachma and the lost sheep and the prodigal son, all these parables say the same thing. Christ said, "There will be more rejoicing in heaven over one repentant sinner than over ninety-nine virtuous men who have no need of repentance." Doesn't that bring hope? Doesn't it make you throw your guilt out? The message is clear—extra love is poured out on the repentant sinner, the greater the sinner, the greater God's love is poured out and the greater the joy in heaven.

O Lord and Master of my life,
grant that I may not be infected
with the spirit of sloth, faintheartedness,
ambition, and idle talk,
but give instead to me your servant
the spirit of purity, humility,
patience, and love.
O Lord and King,
grant me the grace to see my own sins
and not to judge my brother,
for you are blessed forever.
Amen

(Prayer of St. Ephraim the Syrian).

Chapter Three

Penance

My children,
our love is not to be just words or mere talk,
but something real and active;
only by this can we be certain
that we are children of the truth
and be able to quiet our conscience
in his presence.

1 John 3:18,19

Jesus, I'm Sorry

Jesus' call to conversion and penance…does not aim
first at outward works, "sackcloth and ashes," fasting
and mortification, but at the conversion of the heart,
interior conversion. Without this, such penances
remain sterile and false; however, interior conversion
urges expression in visible signs, gestures, and works
of penance (Catechism of the Catholic Church,
1430).

How is repentance brought to God?

Normally, for Catholics, the channel to grace is confession.

Repentance comes, the cry comes out of our heart, and we go to confession. We go to the man God has appointed and share our sins.

If you cannot reach a priest, if you live on an island all by yourself, or if you are somewhere far away where priests cannot come, or if you are alone when you are dying, you don't have to go to a priest to confess. If you live in Timbuktu where there is no priest or somewhere where a priest comes once a year, well, talk to God and he will absolve you; and when the priest comes, talk to him about it. It's so simple.

The person who listens to your confession has one job: first, to love and to give the kiss of Christ and his mercy and forgiveness and so forth; and secondly, to lead you to God in ever-mounting steps. "The confessor is not the master of God's forgiveness, but its servant. The minister of this sacrament should unite himself to the intention and charity of Christ. He should have a proven knowledge of Christian behavior, experience of human affairs, respect and sensitivity toward the one who has fallen; he must love the truth, be faithful to the Magisterium of the Church, and lead the penitent with patience toward healing and full maturity. He must pray and do penance for his penitent, entrusting him to the Lord's mercy" (*Catechism*, 1466). He becomes, as it were, the Jesus Christ who says, "Come higher, friend." But, of course, he is not God, and he says, "Take my hand and let's go higher toward Jesus Christ."

When I was young, my mother had a very precious cup that she had left on the table. She said to me, "Catherine, don't touch this cup. Don't break it. It's a precious cup."

Now at the age of five or so, that begins to be interesting. So I circled around the table for awhile. Then, finally, I picked it up, and eventually it broke. So I thought it over and put it into a wastebasket, considering that what you don't see, you might forget.

When mother came back and looked, there was no cup on the table, and she asked, "Catherine, did you touch the cup?"

At this point, I felt that it wasn't right to have done all those things, and something in me said that I had better confess and tell her how sorry I was. So I did, and my mother put me on her lap and said, "I'm glad you have been truthful and are sorry. You are a good little girl. Let's kiss one another. I forgive you. It's okay. But you broke the cup, didn't you?"

I said, "Yes."

She said, "Well, you have to pay a little for it. So you will give me two cents a week from your allowance, so that you know there are certain things you have to repair."

Now wasn't that just? And it reminded me not to break other cups.

Sacramental confession is you coming to God and saying, "I am really sorry about that broken cup. Here I am, I confess it, and I am in full repentance about it."

And God embraces you, again.

My going and apologizing to the cook about my mother's cup wouldn't get me any place in my mother's heart. I had to talk to my mother, to the person to whom this cup belonged—the same with confession. This is why personal confession, eyeball to eyeball, instead of only general confession, is important.

To me, in my deep faith, a priest is Christ when he is exercising his powers. I kneel before the priest, but, in my mind, it is Christ. When I kneel and tell him, "Forgive me, Lord," quietly, deeply, Christ kisses my forehead and says, "I absolve you," and then I am absolutely clean. Sinless, at least, for the moment. And all is well with me.

I have to do some penance, it stands to reason. But the unforgettable thought alone remains: God loved the world so much that he sent his only Son into our midst, and at a price of great suffering of his Son, reconciled us with himself (Jn 3:16).

Because he did so, joy springs forth, joy that you barely can catch. That joy is there when you kneel and say, "Lord, I am sorry." The forgiveness of God in his most Holy Trinity covers you.

Forgetting God

"Even when he disobeyed you and lost your friend-ship you did not abandon him to the power of death.... Again and again you offered a covenant to man" (Eucharistic Prayer IV, Catechism of the Catholic Church, 55).

What is sin?

One of our priests was explaining today at Mass that the word sin means "forgetting" in Hebrew. It's a very good definition of sin. "The Holy Spirit is the Church's living memory" (*Catechism*, 1099). But sin means forgetting God—separating from him, turning our backs toward him.

With God, every moment is the moment of beginning again, yet, when we sin, we refuse to believe that. Sin is getting outside of something beautiful, something that is healing, something that is renewing. We reject God as the Pharisees and a lot of other people he knew rejected him.

Sin is to tear yourself away from the embrace of God. "Sin is before all else an offense against God, a rupture of communion with him." "Sin sets itself against God's love for us and turns our hearts away from it" (*Catechism*, 1440, 1850). It's not a question of fear of hell. It is a question of love and rejection of love. It might have nothing to do with an act. It might have something to do with the interior you, the unfaithfulness to the Beloved in a thousand ways that are not visible to the naked eye. Any sin offends the majesty and goodness of God and breaks the bond of love.

Anything that goes against love is sin. St. Augustine said, "Love and do what you will," because if you love, you won't hurt anybody. All sins are against charity. The greatest sin is not to love. All the others flow from that sin, the sin of *uncharity.*

If you want to go to bed with a woman and she isn't your wife, or you want to go to bed with a man and he isn't your husband, that it is a sin against charity. It is a sin of disrespect of one another. If you really love somebody, you don't go to bed with him. You wait until the blessing of God is upon your love.

If you steal something, it is against charity. You have deprived someone of his or her goods, and that is uncharitable.

If you murder someone, that is very uncharitable.

All sins, no matter how small or how big, mortal or venial, break love in some way. "Charity keeps the commandments of God and his Christ: 'Abide in my love. If you keep my commandments, you will abide in my love'" (*Catechism*, 1824). Sin breaks my love toward God. And that is tragic.

To sin is to lose God. A mortal sin cuts us off from his friendship, with a sharp cut. To sin mortally is also to move from light into darkness, and in the darkness one loses one's way.

This is what has happened to our generation. We have gone so far as even to deny that there is sin and that there is One against whom we can sin. Because of just such a denial—on a grand scale, peace, happiness, and joy, the fruits of justice and charity, which have their roots in God himself, have fled our frightened world. We stand apart from God shivering in the dark and the cold. Over the whole world, whether we know it or not, the strange pall of sin falls like a dark fog, and we are walking through it. No wonder we are full of fears.

If we Catholics, who are the salt of the earth, are to restore the world to Christ, then we must do so with clean souls, clean minds, clean hands. "Charity upholds and purifies our human ability to love, and raises it to the supernatural perfection of divine love" (*Catechism*, 1827). As years go by, living a life of love and of prayer will make us sensitive to ever-changing needs and hence to the signs of God in our lives.

God is close to us and his angel will come down to stir the quiet waters of a conscience that as yet does not quite understand, is too young to make right judgments. A sensitive, Christian conscience may feel "sickened" by or have an emotional reaction to sin. Love gives us a delicate conscience that desires to regularly reexamine our lives before his face.

We must realize, first, the tragedy that sin is. And then, with tears of repentance, we must purify ourselves in the most holy sacrament of Penance.

But man, being what he is, or she is, falls along the narrow road, for temptations, like boulders, are strewn on the path. I go to confession, make resolutions, and then break them again and again. Confronted with a mountain of defects, I have been tempted to give up trying. But then, I remember that Christ dwells in my heart and is "compelled" to live in the disorder there, and I begin again to try and clean my heart, with his help. We say, "Lord, kiss our sins away."

The saddest thing in the world is to be alienated from God. Sin is a terrible thing, an alienation from God, as if I cut with a knife his tenderness, his love. I reject all that he covers me with—*I*, not he.

He will still be there, though, even if I have rejected everything. You might leave the Church, but the Church hasn't left you. That is the great difference. Christ hasn't left you. Christ came to restore sinners. "Christ died out of love for us, while we were still 'enemies'" (*Catechism*, 1825). He became the one who took all our sins upon his shoulders. So we are the beloved, his beloved, the ones he rescued from sin.

Because sinning means forgetting God, repentance is simply a statement of how you feel, in faith, about having forgotten. For Catholics, the channel to grace is normally the sacrament of confession or Reconciliation. The cry of repentance comes out of our heart and we go to confession.

It is so simple. It is just one confession. "The confession or disclosure of sins, even from a simply human point of view, frees us and facilitates our reconciliation with others. Through such an admission, man looks squarely at the sins he is guilty of, takes responsibility for them, and thereby opens himself to God (*Catechism*, 1455).

It is like a dirge in your soul that rises and sings its lament, "Father, I have sinned against love." Let us run into God's arms and make up.

Free and Happy

The practice of the moral life animated by charity gives to the Christian the spiritual freedom of the children of God. He no longer stands before God as a slave, in servile fear, or as a mercenary looking for wages, but as a son responding to the love of him who "first loved us" (Catechism of the Catholic Church, 1828).

The greatest thing that we have is free will. We can sin, and we can not sin. We can do good, and we can do evil, and that makes the difference between us and all the rest of creation.

"God created man a rational being, conferring on him the dignity of a person who can initiate and control his own actions. 'God willed that man should be "left in the hand of his own counsel," so that he might of his own accord seek his Creator and freely attain his full and blessed perfection by cleaving to him'" (*Catechism*, 1730).

The amazing part is that God, in his infinite mercy, took the power that he had, for God is all-powerful, and simply restrained it, in regard to man. He gave man the commandment of love, and he left him free to practice or not to practice it. It is up to you. You don't have to. Nobody puts a pistol to your head. "If you wish you can keep the commandments. They are within your power" (Eccl 15:15). You can do whatever you like, and that is the miracle of God's goodness, of God's mercy, and the strange, incomprehensible respect that he has towards man.

The psalmist says, "What is man that you should keep him in mind, mortal man that you care for him?" (Ps 8:5). He is just a speck on the horizon before the Lord. Yet what more can you ask of God than to withhold his power? He could annihilate us in a second. He could make us slaves in a minute if he wanted to, so that we would act like little puppets, but he didn't do any of those things. He left us free. This is the most beautiful thing in the world—to be free before God—to choose between good and evil. God has created you in his image. "Man is rational and therefore like God; he is created with free will and is master over his acts" (St. Irenaeus, *Catechism*, 1730). God has allowed you to choose—and to know that he is also there to help.

"The grace of Christ is not in the slightest way a rival of our freedom when this freedom accords with the sense of the true and the good that God has put in the human heart. On the contrary, as Christian experience attests especially in prayer, the more docile we are to the promptings of grace, the more we grow in inner freedom and confidence during trials, such as those we face in the pressures and constraints of the outer world.

By the working of grace, the Holy Spirit educates us in spiritual freedom" (*Catechism*, 1742).

We examine sin usually from the moral aspect. That is a good place to start, because ethics and morality are with us, whether we're Christians or non-Christians. For Christians, it goes deeper. Sin is my rejection of God. I simply say to God, "Look, I am tired of your commandments and what you eternally ask of me in the name of love. I want to do what I want to do, when I want to do it, and how I want to do it. And I don't want you to dictate anything to me."

We find ourselves "free" to do what we want to do, as we want to do it, when we want to do it. Then, begins a great tragedy within our soul, because we find that we are absolutely tired out. "The exercise of freedom does not imply a right to say or do everything" (*Catechism*, 1740). Doing what you want, as you want, when you want, doesn't seem to be exactly what you thought it was. "Man failed. He freely sinned. By refusing God's plan of love, he deceived himself and became a slave to sin. This first alienation engendered a multitude of others" (*Catechism*, 1739). You enter into something that makes you thoroughly unhappy.

Stainless must be our wedding garment when we come before the gaze of the Bridegroom. We can keep it white and pure from baptism to death, for his grace is always there to help us.

But we are weak, weighed down with the flesh, the world, and the devil. We fall and stain our baptismal robes. Oh, the goodness of God! They can be washed clean, and for this he offers us the confessional, where, in utter abandonment of love, he washes them with his own Precious Blood. All that remains to us then, is to make up here and now, in this world, on this earth, the penance given to us by him through his priest.

"Happy are those who mourn: they shall be comforted" (Mt 5:5). Meditate and besiege the Lord for tears of repentance to wash the stain of all sin, mortal and venial, from our souls. This is the acceptable time to mourn over our sins. To do penance and to pray. To fast. To wear sackcloth and ashes—if not factually, at least, spiritually.

Repentance is a flame that comes out of your heart. You have hurt somebody. And this person is God. You come to him and say, "Look, Jesus, I am sorry, I really mean it. You get the picture: I mean it." You go to confession, and get his kiss, and you get absolution, and you walk out, and you feel happy.

Christ bends and kisses you. The kiss of Christ is the pain of Christ, but the kiss is also the freedom of Christ. "By his glorious Cross Christ has won salvation for all men. He redeemed them from the sin that held them in bondage. 'For freedom Christ has set us free.' In him we have communion with the 'truth that makes us free.' The Holy Spirit has been given to us and, as the Apostle teaches, 'Where the Spirit of the Lord is, there is freedom.' Already we glory in the 'liberty of the children of God'" (*Catechism*, 1741).

There is a tremendous grace conferred onto a person who confesses often. Strength comes to that person, to eschew sins. "Indeed the regular confession of our venial sins helps us form our conscience, fight against evil tendencies, let ourselves be healed by Christ, and progress in the life of the Spirit" (*Catechism*, 1458).

Confession is mercy. When I open my heart in confession and say, "Lord, I have sinned against love, have mercy on me," down comes this mercy, and you return to being a child of God.

All the Sadness in the World

Conversion of heart is accompanied by a salutary pain and sadness (Catechism of the Catholic Church, *1431*).

It is incredible that a Christian should continue to feel guilty after confession. I can understand that he feels exceedingly sad. I can understand when he feels like crying. Russians pray for the gift of tears, because the tears wash guilt away, among other things.

How can I remain guilty when I am pardoned the moment I say that I am sorry? That I can feel the alienation between myself and Christ, sure. When I remove myself from Christ because I have sinned, then all the sadness of the world can come into my heart, but guilt cannot linger there.

How can I forget that God is merciful? I explained to God that I would like to have five minutes of guilt as many feel it, so that I could come to them and say, "Oh yes, now I know how you feel." But I don't know how to be guilty. I know how to weep. I know how to be sad. I know how to cry in the night. But I don't know how to be guilty, because there is a gospel. And all guilt is covered by the mercy of God.

Across the centuries a voice says, "Do not judge, and you will not be judged." (Mt 7:1). How can one read the gospel and doubt the mercy of God?

You who cry in the night and who weep in the day, be at peace. Be at peace. Whatever guilt there has been, he has risen and his blood has washed it away. You can come to him and make a cup out of your hands, and one drop of this blood, symbolically, will clean you, if you have faith in his mercy. And if you say four little words: "Lord, I am sorry."

Of course, if you have mortal sin on your soul, go to a priest, because Christ gave priests the key. When we confess a grave sin, hope should surge in us, not guilt that leads to despondency, anger, and despair, but hope, like a light, like a song.

Lingering guilt should be totally alien to the Christian if he has faith. For if he has faith, he knows the mercy of God. Let us lay guilt aside. Christ is in our midst. Believe, and nothing that could happen to you or me in this world makes any difference. The advocate, the helper of the poor, is by my side. What have I to fear? Nothing. When you are not filled with guilt, you can begin to think about the mercy of God and a lot of other things that you can pass on to others to the best of your ability.

Don't hold on to your guilt. Set your doubts aside. Put all that in a bundle and throw it out. Here is faith, that belief stronger than death. It is as if hail were falling on the roof, and we are all warm inside. There is hail on the roof, but in your heart there is a flame, and in your soul there is love that is stronger than death.

A Christian can have sorrow, a gentle sorrow, and a new prayer for faith not to commit the sin done before. "The interior penance of the Christian can be expressed in many and various ways. Scripture and the Fathers insist above all on three forms, *fasting, prayer, and almsgiving,* which express conversion in relation to oneself, to God, and to others. Alongside the radical purification brought about by Baptism or martyrdom, they cite as means of obtaining forgiveness of sins: efforts at reconciliation with one's neighbor, tears of repentance, concern for the salvation of one's neighbor, the intercession of the saints, and the practice of charity 'which covers a multitude of sins'" (*Catechism*, 1434).

Let us pray for the gift of tears. Let us pray for the gift of love, so as not to sin. Let us pray for simplicity, the simplicity of a child who has just broken Mama's favorite cup and runs into her arms and says, "I am sorry."

How to Examine and Form Your Conscience

The reception of this sacrament ought to be prepared for by an examination of conscience made in the light of the Word of God (Catechism of the Catholic Church, 1454).

What does it mean to examine one's conscience?

To examine one's conscience means to recollect oneself—to *collect* all the fragments.

You have to become still, not allow your heart or mind to be buzzing like flies. In total stillness, with firm resolve, you descend into your heart; there, you find what has to be thrown out.

A holy and good examination of your conscience and yourself, naturally, becomes a time of tension and questioning. Sins against charity, of pride, of indifference to others—to my brothers and sisters—these sins bite. In a way, this searching may lead, from the worldly point of view, to dire consequences, for it may revolutionize your life.

A searching examination of conscience must be undertaken. We can and should face ourselves and make an examination of conscience, find those sins of omission and commission against our vocation to love. We have to examine our consciences for every little compromise, every rationalization. It has to be a thorough examination, without self-illusion, without compromise.

Since you must face yourself and see yourself as clearly as is humanly possible, an examination of conscience must begin with fervent prayer.

Let us examine our consciences:

The first point of an examination of conscience should be on sins against love—How much do I love?

In selfishness, we have a simple yardstick of love. Most of the things that have to be thrown out deal with selfishness. How often in my life does the pronoun *I* disappear, replaced by *they, we, he*, or *she*? Let's say a thought comes to mind, "I want to do this." If it is something God would like you to do, do it. If not, erase it, and keep on erasing it. The *I* will disappear, and someday, perhaps, we will kneel and kiss the feet of somebody else.

How do I betray Jesus?

So many of us are Judases, betraying Christ with a kiss, so to speak. It's a subtle thing. I think it's one of the grave sins. People worry about sex sins. Sex has been created by God, but pride, arrogance, and those sort of things, have not been created by God. We should examine our conscience deeply, because our betrayals are so subtle, and this sort of sin escapes us so quickly. We water down, rationalize, find excuses for not doing what we know we should.

How far away from God am I? Why?

Let us look into our own hearts. Where has my heart wandered? Christ said "Be perfect just as your heavenly Father is perfect" (Mt 5:48). In Baptism, the little feet begin the journey of union with God. He calls us to give the whole of ourselves. He calls us to perfection. In Russia, we have no distinction between a Trappist and a father of a family, between a married woman and a Trappistine, because we believe that Christ said, "Be perfect," to everybody.

To what places has my heart gone?

When we discuss the gospel, we have an ability to rationalize. Intellectual seduction is one of the greatest sins. To take faith and break it, to rationalize away from Christ, so as to make another person feel like you do, to rationalize away from the Lord's commandment to love, is terrible. And those are the sins that are walking amongst us today, literally walking and calling, like some kind of a siren, calling us betray our very profound beliefs.

We make believe that we're Catholics. We talk about the scriptures, but the scriptures are empty words unless you put them into practice. It's useless to listen and do nothing. It will be held against you if you know the scriptures and don't apply them. The gospel is limpidly clear. It's addressed to ordinary people—you and me. Look deep down into your soul, see what's wrong, throw it out, bring Christ in. There is so little time.

"Am I my brother's keeper?"

We keep repeating the words of Cain (Gn 4:9). Before this constantly repeated answer of man to God there is only one place we can go: into the emptiness of our inner desert, there to face ourselves, to examine our consciences which have been so seemingly totally asleep.

Why don't I make a clean sweep?

See the mess that is in your heart. Bring it all out. Our confessions can be superficial and not go deep enough. If they are superficial, we haven't really gone into the caverns and caves of our souls. We've wrapped a lot of things in cellophane and stuck them on the shelves, when they should have been brought forth. But we let them be, and like splinters they fester in our soul. We are not in truth, and we have left integrity behind somewhere.

Thirty-three years of lecturing are now behind me. And when I try to remember their content, I do not have to strain my memory, for all of them had but one theme. All called upon audiences to wake up from their sleep of complacency, to examine their consciences. Let us make a point to examine our consciences nightly. We must resort to the sackcloth and ashes of repentance. We must examine our consciences, turn our faces to God and heed the voice of his vicar.

But what's the use of talking about it if I haven't developed a conscience? And how does one develop one's conscience? That's very simple. We go back to love again. Through concern for the other, we become aware of a lot of things. Let us work on our faults, on our sins of omission and commission. Let us be watchful over them, so as to eliminate them. Be ready to have prickings of conscience constantly; these prickings will function to develop in you a very delicate conscience.

Parents are the primary teachers of the spiritual life of their children. Formation of conscience must come through parents whose own consciences are delicately formed, and who can transmit that delicacy to their children. From the parents, the child absorbs the power to distinguish between good and evil, the ability to examine his or her conscience openly and in peace. From the parents, the child acquires the understanding of Christ's infinite mercy and love.

You see yourself, but never despair, because along with your sins, you see the mercy of God. You look at yourself. You realize the depth and the breadth of sin. Then, you look at God and say, "Lord, have mercy on me." In the process, you forget yourself. You begin to contemplate God, and all else disappears in him.

Let's work on our consciences, in prayer, in deep prayer. For prayer alone will overcome our little faults and big ones, and give us the courage to do that which has to be done, so that we might begin, at least, to say, with St. Paul, "I live now not with my own life but with the life of Christ who lives in me" (Gal 2:20).

Beloved,
it is indeed clear to me
that what you desire of me
is to fight myself,
because my first duty
is to save myself—
my immortal soul—
and that means a continual fight.

Please, teach me
to go about it in the right way,
to listen carefully to my conscience,
to understand it is your voice
quietly speaking to me.
I am yours, Jesus,
with all my will,
but my senses are strong.
They fight my will.
Help me.
Amen.

Chapter Four

Confession

*Until they confess their guilt and seek my face,
they will search for me in their misery.*

Hosea 5:15

Whatever Became of Sin

*"God wrote on the tables of the Law what men did
not read in their hearts"* (St. Augustine, Catechism
of the Catholic Church, 1962).

In the sixties, through hippies, intellectuals, lib-
erals, and others, we began to excuse sin. The
sense of sin has almost disappeared. Sin is called
anything but "sin." People sin and don't know
that they're sinning.

There is an interesting book called *Whatever
Became of Sin,* by Dr. Karl Menninger. He found
that people who had been supposedly liberated
by psychiatrists became worse off later on. There
was no healing through eliminating the notion of
sin.

I remember the sixties. Hippies were going around saying that there is no God, falling into everybody's bed, doing anything they wanted. If you mentioned the word "sin," they laughed. But strangely enough, if you were listening with your heart—not only your ears—you heard them cry. You just can't push things around like that, because sin exists. It's a reality. The lines got blurred. We have to watch out for that if we are to be instruments of God's healing.

"The apostle John says, 'If we say we have no sin, we deceive ourselves, and the truth is not in us.'" "All members of the Church, including her ministers, must acknowledge that they are sinners" (*Catechism*, 1425, 827). Let's face it. We cannot love the way we ought to. We are used to our anxiety. We are secure in our selfishness. We do not want to mature, to accept the awesome, terrible, totally liberating freedom that comes when we enter the law of love that God gives us.

Christ asks us to depart, with his grace, from our selfish existence. You will falter, you will stumble, you will fall. But don't stay down. Don't compromise. Keep cooperating with the graces God gives you. "This is the struggle of *conversion* directed toward holiness and eternal life to which the Lord never ceases to call us" (*Catechism*, 1426).

"Whoever confesses his sins…is already working with God. God indicts your sins; if you also indict them, you are joined with God" (*Catechism*, 1458). In those yesterdays of mine, the typical Russian would never deny that sin is a sin. He would not excuse a sin. He would say that adultery is adultery, and I have committed adultery. Fornication is fornication, and I have committed fornication. Lying is lying, and I have lied. Stealing is stealing, and I have stolen. "When you begin to abhor [the reality that] you have made, it is then that your good works are beginning, since you are accusing yourself of your evil works. The beginning of good works is the confession of evil works. You do the truth and come to the light" (St. Augustine, *Catechism* 1458).

Love, cherish, and heal the sinner, for God came for sinners. "Christ instituted the sacrament of Penance for all sinful members of his Church: above all for those who, since Baptism, have fallen into grave sin, and have thus lost their baptismal grace and wounded ecclesial communion. It is to them that the sacrament of Penance offers a new possibility to convert and to recover the grace of justification" (*Catechism*, 1446).

But, put squarely before people what sin is and never condone it. "If they live her life [the Church], her members are sanctified; if they move away from her life, they fall into sins and disorders that prevent the radiation of her sanctity" (*Catechism*, 827).

We can *never* condone sin, but we must *always* love the sinner. It is as simple as that. "In everyone, the weeds of sin will still be mixed with good wheat of the gospel until the end of time" (*Catechism*, 827).

In the hippie days, a girl came to me and said that she had slept with forty-eight men. It was one of those crazy experiments. When we talked about it, two aspects of the situation struck me. First, she was pushed into this by her peers. She was innocent when she left home for college, a Catholic college. She was egged on by her Catholic friends. Secondly, Mama warned her too much. She was exceedingly frightened of sex.

We discussed all this—what was her sin, what was not her sin, what was the sin of Mama, what was the sin of the kids who pushed her. Finally, I said, "How do you feel?"

"Like a secondhand piece of goods, sold in some lousy basement on some tenement street," she said.

She knew perfectly well that it was not before her mother or her peers that she was ultimately guilty. That's when she fell on her knees, put her head in my lap, and started crying, because she knew she was guilty before God.

I said, "Go to confession to receive the kiss of Christ. That will erase all those evil kisses you have received through the years, for God is merciful."

You Were Created for Love

"Love is itself the fulfillment of all our works. There is the goal; that is why we run: we run toward it, and once we reach it, in it we shall find rest" (St. Augustine, Catechism of the Catholic Church, 1829).

If I sin grievously, my sin is not a private affair. It affects everyone, every Catholic in the world, for it tears the Mystical Body of Christ.

And then again, what is sin?

The means of grace and salvation, the objects of hope—are found in the sacraments. What we must avoid if we would be saved—the things that belong to charity—are contained in the commandments of God. The ways of perfection are clear—the Commandments, the Beatitudes, the Counsels. The Ten Commandments were given to us to keep us away from sin—original sin, venial sin, mortal sin.

From original sin, we inherited a certain darkness of mind, a certain weakness of will, that even the holy water of Baptism did not wash completely away, and we resolved to pray to the good Lord for the grace always to fight and watch these weaknesses.

Sin, even venial sin, is an offense against God. Venial sins, those sly, wispy, little actions, are always beckoning to us to sidestep the straight and lovely path God made for us. "When the sinner's will is set upon something that of its nature involves a disorder, but is not opposed to the love of God and neighbor, such as thoughtless chatter or immoderate laughter and the like, such sins are venial" (St. Thomas Aquinas, *Catechism*, 1856).

Venial sins are harbingers, not of spring, but of dark forbidding storms to come—heralds of temptations, that once yielded to, weaken the guardians of our souls—our wills. How earnestly we must guard against sins, how constantly we must pray for strength and vigilance!

I came across a little diary I wrote when I was thirteen years old, and I was horrified to see that the same weaknesses and sins I struggled against, then, almost semi-consciously, I struggle against today. A lifetime of futile efforts. I turn inward and go into the shadowy depths of my own soul, seeking there the sins of omission and commission that have escaped the vigilance of years.

The greatest tragedy in the world is mortal sin. Yet how few of us realize it. To sin is to die. To sin is to be empty.

Mortal sin, which is not spoken of today, is an offense against God. "When the will sets itself upon something that is of its nature incompatible with the charity that orients man toward his ultimate end, then the sin is mortal by its very object...whether it contradicts the love of God, such as blasphemy or perjury, or the love of neighbor, such as homicide or adultery" (St. Thomas Aquinas, *Catechism*, 1856).

Yet there is a more personal result of mortal sin. The Way of the Cross, in any Catholic Church, no matter how inartistic, no matter how garish the Stations may be, vividly depicts *our* betrayal. For Christ, there is no time. Your sin and mine contributed to his *Via Dolorosa*—to every step of it. A sorrowful, tragic thought—yet a wholesome one in these days when the fruit of sin is ripening under the sun of hell all about us.

Mortal sin not only kills our soul, it crucifies love, and love is God, and God is love. Think of it, friend, you and I, executioners of Christ. The real guilt of mortal sin, if not confessed, becomes like a cancer eating up one's heart and soul. It upsets the equilibrium of the entire person. "Mortal sin, by attacking the vital principle within us—that is, charity—necessitates a new initiative of God's mercy and a conversion of heart which is normally accomplished within the setting of the sacrament of Reconciliation." "The Fathers of the Church present this sacrament as 'the second plank [of salvation] after the shipwreck which is the loss of grace'" (*Catechism*, 1856, 1446).

During the relaxing hours in bed, my mind goes to an examination of conscience. Once in a while, I take time off and examine every part of my life. Thus, all I need at night is a sort of a general glance on the whole of my day, on each of its parts. If I failed, I try to find out why, and act accordingly. I examine how deeply integrated my day has been, how pure my intention. It comes back to the idea that sanctity is the unity of my will with God's, in love.

Then, I muster all my will and intellect, and go to a confessor and confess my sins. For that alone can achieve the desired effect. "When Christ's faithful strive to confess all the sins that they can remember, they undoubtedly place all of them before the divine mercy for pardon" (*Catechism*, 1456). In regard to the sacrament of Reconciliation, we Russians use the words "enfolded in the love of Christ."

In everyday terms, we ordinarily call "sins" those of the flesh. But what of those of the spirit? What of those inner movements so hidden, so deep that seem to whisper, "You are okay; do not bestir yourself; you *are* doing enough; there is no need to do more."? What yesterday seemed to be virtue, today, in the pitiless brilliant light of the Holy Spirit's fire, looks drab and almost sinful. What yesterday seemed natural and permissible, today, with a new-given grace, looks weak and cowardly.

What of the lack of charity toward one's neighbor in thought and speech? What of that impatience and almost criticism of the hierarchy that comes in such desperate waves and, for all that remains unuttered, is still there before God?

To enter into heaven, we must be saints; either now, or later through much suffering and pain in purgatory. Why delay? Why not start now?

Sanctity does not imply only fasting, only penance. It means *much loving*. That is what we have been created for, to love—to love our neighbor and, through him, God. Learn how to love, and all the rest will be added unto you.

A Humbled, Contrite Heart

It is in discovering the greatness of God's love that our heart is shaken by the horror and weight of sin and begins to fear offending God by sin and being separated from him (Catechism of the Catholic Church, 1432).

David acknowledged his sins. That was his greatest claim to fame.

He fell in love with a woman who had a husband who was an army officer. "It happened toward evening when David had risen from his couch and was strolling on the palace roof, that he saw from the roof a woman bathing; the woman was very beautiful. David made inquiries about this woman and was told...'That is Bathsheba...the wife of Uriah the Hittite.'

"Then David sent messengers and had her brought. She came to him, and he slept with her.

"She then went home again. The woman conceived and sent word to David, 'I am with child.'

"Then David sent Joab a message, 'Send me Uriah.'

"When Uriah came into his presence, David asked after Joab and the army and how the war was going. David then said to Uriah, 'Go down to your house and enjoy yourself.' Uriah however slept by the palace door...and did not go down to his house."

"This was reported to David.

"So David asked Uriah, 'Have you not just arrived from a journey? Why do you not go to your home?' But Uriah answered, 'Are not the ark and the men of Israel and Judah lodged in tents; and my master Joab and the bodyguard of my lord, are they not in the open fields? Am I to go to my house, then, and eat and drink and sleep with my wife? As the Lord lives, and as you yourself live, I will do no such thing!'" (2 Sm 11:2–13).

So, David sent Uriah far away to be killed, and David lived with the woman.

"David wrote a letter to Joab and sent it by Uriah. In the letter he wrote, 'Station Uriah in the thick of the fight and then fall back behind him so that he may be struck down and die'" (2 Sm 11:14–15).

"When Uriah's wife heard that her husband Uriah was dead, she mourned for her husband. When the period of mourning was over, David sent to have her brought to his house; she became his wife and bore him a son. But what David had done displeased the Lord" (2 Sm 11:26–27).

"The Lord sent Nathan the prophet to David. He came to him and said:

"'In the same town were two men, one rich, the other poor. The rich man had flocks and herds in great abundance; the poor man had nothing but a ewe lamb, one only, a small one he had bought. This he fed, and it grew up with him and his children, eating his bread, drinking from his cup, sleeping on his breast; it was like a daughter to him. When there came a traveler to stay, the rich man refused to take one of his own flock or herd to provide for the wayfarer who had come to him. Instead he took the poor man's lamb and prepared it for his guest.'

"David's anger flared up against the man" (2 Sm 12:1–4).

"Nathan said to David, 'You are the man. The Lord the God of Israel says this, "I anointed you…I delivered you…I gave your master's house to you…I gave you the House of Israel and Judah; and if this were not enough, I would add as much again for you. Why have you shown contempt for the Lord, doing what displeases him? You have struck down Uriah…and taken the wife of Uriah the Hittite to be your wife"' (2 Sm 12:7–12).

"David said to Nathan, 'I have sinned against the Lord'" (2 Sm 12:13).

One of the Psalms mentions how David repented, loudly and brilliantly. "Have mercy on me, God, in your kindness. In your compassion blot out my offense. O wash me more and more from my guilt and cleanse me from my sin.…A pure heart create for me, O God, put a steadfast spirit within me. Do not cast me away from your presence, nor deprive me of your Holy Spirit. Give me again the joy of your help.…O rescue me, God, my helper, and my tongue shall ring out your goodness. O Lord, open my lips and my mouth shall declare your praise.…My sacrifice, a contrite spirit; a humbled, contrite heart you will not spurn" (Ps 50).

That kind of person should be close to us.

"Nathan said to David, 'The Lord, for his part, forgives your sin'" (2 Sm 12:14).

Fear and Loathing

"If the sick person is too ashamed to show his wound to the doctor, the medicine cannot heal what it does not know" (St. Jerome, Catechism of the Catholic Church, 1456).

I was astonished when I found that people are afraid of confession. Who is afraid of being kissed by Christ? Who can be afraid when he knows he is held tenderly in the hands of Jesus Christ?

Let's look at sin. The wrong idea of sin is deeply ingrained in so many people. People are afraid when they talk about sin. A sort of panic gets hold of them. Sin seems to be sort of a mirror that changes them. Like in a carnival midway, you look in one mirror and you are fat, you look in another mirror and you are thin. The idea of sin seems to change a person. They think of themselves as ugly, unpleasant, unlovable, because they say to themselves that they are sinful. Then, the spiritual malady, spiritual fear, translates itself into a psychological fear, which means that we believe that we're unlovable.

One way or another, fear is a weapon of the devil. We were created to be saints. But Satan laughs and hopes to confuse even those who were baptized and promised to renounce the works and pomps of Satan.

Fear is exorcised by two things—prayer and the forgiveness of those who have done us harm. But first forgive yourself. I think if you really forgive yourself, you will have peace, the peace that surpasses all understanding.

Where love is, there cannot be fear. The Lord died on a cross, the Lord resurrected and ascended. What for? To save us. To reconcile us with his Father. I wish that all Christians thought of themselves as *saved sinners*, because they are.

You Look Like Your Father

"If we confess our sins, he is faithful and just, and will forgive our sins and cleanse us from all unrighteousness" (1 Jn 1:9, Catechism of the Catholic Church, 1847).

No matter who we are and what we are, the mercy of God is given to us.

Do we or don't we believe in his mercy?

Do we face that what comes out of the hands of God cannot be ugly, deformed, lousy?

How can you have a wrong image of yourself when you know that you come from the hands of the loving God?

Look at your face in a mirror, and you see *God's image:* "In so far as you did this to one of the least of these brothers of mine, you did it to *me*" (Mt 25:40, emphasis added). Why do we pull ourselves down? Why are we worried? Why are we trying to get people to approve of us?

Have we forgotten that we were created and loved by God himself? Have we forgotten the Incarnation? The Crucifixion? The Resurrection? The Ascension? Have we forgotten the mercy of God?

Do you feel the warmth of God's mercy? Do you feel the tenderness that embraces you? Do you hear that knock at your heart that says, "You don't need to be lonely and worried about this. I am with you. I am in you. I am among you."

Do you feel his consolation? Not in any psychological sense, I mean in a spiritual sense, in faith. Do you feel the touch of his hand upon your heart, healing the wound you have made through sin?

We are human. Unfortunately, we are likely to sin in one way or another. It will take us a long time to get over it. But in the moment we have sinned—that very moment—we should cry out to God, "Lord, have mercy," and then go to confession about it.

Don't let sin twist you. Don't let the one who induces you into sin make you feel that you're cut off from God because you sinned. Tell Satan, "Go where you belong and stay there."

Confess, "I have sinned. I'm sorry. Lord, have mercy on me." And listen to the devil sizzle as he goes down. Just listen to him sizzle. The moment you say, "Lord, have mercy," Satan disappears.

You may say that this is an almost infantile approach to sin. I don't think so. It's an approach in faith, the great and deep faith that God alone can give us, and for which we must pray. Faith alone can cure this wrong image of sin, this fear. It comes down to faith.

Faith believes unshakably in the mercy of God and realizes that, unless I am merciful, I shall not find mercy. If I believe God is merciful, then out of the depths of my soul, comes my mercy, which is his, given to everyone. "By receiving more frequently through this sacrament the gift of the Father's mercy, we are spurred to be merciful as he is merciful" (*Catechism*, 1458). Have you ever experienced the mercy of someone? If you ever have experienced it, you know its tenderness and warmth.

If anyone of us sins, again, let us be peaceful about it, sorrowful and sad, but also filled with gratitude that we are able to say, "Lord, have mercy," and then receive his mercy.

That doesn't mean that we should go around saying, "Well, because he's merciful, I'm going to sin." No, on the contrary, say, "Because he's merciful, I shall be merciful" (Rom 6:1–2).

If we have fallen, his hand reaches out, he takes us close to his bosom, and presses us to his heart. God is so simple. We have problems, but God is simple. Go to him like a child.

Lay Down Your Burden

The human heart is heavy and hardened. God must give man a new heart (Catechism of the Catholic Church, 1432).

As a member of the Franciscan Third Order in Chicago, I visited a lady. She was in her eighties, all crippled with arthritis, and I used to do her shopping for her. She constantly bemoaned the sinfulness of her youth. I got a little tired of that and picked up my gospel, the one with the pages all curled up. I found Matthew, and I read to her this parable:

"'The kingdom of heaven may be compared to a man who sowed good seed in his field. While everybody was asleep his enemy came and sowed darnel all among the wheat, and made off. When the new wheat sprouted and ripened, the darnel appeared as well. The owner's servants went to him and said, 'Sir, was it not good seed that you sowed in your field? If so, where does the darnel come from?' 'Some enemy has done this,' he answered. And the servants said, 'Do you want us to go and weed it out?' But he said, 'No, because when you weed out the darnel, you might pull up the wheat with it. Let both grow together till harvest; and at harvest time I shall say to the reapers: First collect the darnel and tie it in bundles to be burned, then gather the wheat into my barn'" (Mt 13:24–30).

I said to her, "So maybe you were a bad weed in your youth, and that was too bad. But there's one consolation you have in being darnel: you grew side by side with wheat. So all you have to do now is pray to God to change you into wheat."

We talked about it again and again and again. She said, "Do you think it's too late for me to be changed into wheat?"

I said, "Not at all."

I knelt down by her bed, and she recited the following prayer: "Lord, I didn't even know what darnel was, and, to be absolutely truthful, I still don't. But in your book you say it is a bad thing. That was me. I was darnel when I was young. It reminds me of the darning needles. That's what I associated the word with. But then, I'm old and uneducated. You know what I used to do, Lord? I used to sneak out when my mother was away, and I had fun with the boys. My mother always found out because my darning was always so bad. This lady says that darnel is something else. But you have given me length of days to grow with the wheat."

Then, she turned around to me, "Katie, suppose that you start praying. I've done my praying."

So I turned around to God, and I said, "She wants to be a grain of wheat, just a little grain of wheat, that's all."

Of course, the Lord had no problem with that. He just smiled, lifted his head, and she was changed into wheat.

She said to me, "Look, Katie, I really feel different. Right now, I feel good. I'm wheat."

And she was telling everybody that she was wheat. Some people thought she was crazy.

"'Jesus, remember me when you come into your kingdom.' 'Indeed, I promise you,' he replied, 'today you will be with me in paradise'" (Lk 23:39–43). This word to the good thief is a consolation for all who feel guilty because of their sins. Let guilt be wiped out. If any one of you feels guilty, and you know that you deserve it, fear not. Look at Jesus Christ. You only need to say, "Have mercy on me." Then, with the eyes of faith, see an unseen hand wipe out all your sins and misdemeanors. You will realize you are in paradise because he who is merciful dwells in you. Where he is, there is paradise. It is as simple as that.

After confession of sin, guilt should be totally alien to the Christian who has faith. Faith permits us to know the mercy of God. It enables us

to read and absorb what God said while he was
dying: "Today you will be with me in paradise."

When the burden of sin is unbearable it is
such a relief to go to the sacrament of confession
and lay the burden down at Christ's feet.

Beloved, I contemplate my sins....
The enormity makes me shudder.
Their hideousness is revealed in all its clarity
in the light of your presence.
How little I have done for you!
How mixed my intentions are!
O Beloved, have pity on me, have pity on me.

Jesus, Son of God, I love you
with all the love a poor, broken,
sinful human heart is capable.
 It is exquisite agony to love you, Lord,
because I fall so short.
Like a prisoner stretching his chains
to the breaking point toward freedom,
my soul stretches its arms toward you,
vainly trying to break away
from the shackles of flesh.

O Jesus, Son of God, I adore you
with all my soul, my mind, my body.
I pledge myself to your service
in whatever shape you want.
I am weak,

but with your Holy Spirit at my side,
I hope to be strong even unto death.

Jesus, Son of God, I believe in you
and in all the teachings
of your holy spouse the Church.
I pledge myself to honor you
with her liturgical voice,
to obey her unto death—
to pray for her, to help her.

Jesus Son of God, I am yours now and forever.
If in my weakness I fall, lift me up.
If I fail, encourage me,
for I am weak and alone.
I love, I believe, I adore
your divine will in all things.
Amen.

Chapter Five

Forgiveness

Jesus said…
"My child, your sins are forgiven."

Mark 2:5

The Bright Sadness

"The Spirit helps us in our weakness; for we do not know how to pray as we ought, but the Spirit himself intercedes with sighs too deep for words" (Rom 8:26, Catechism of the Catholic Church, 741).

Repentance, to the West, means sorrow, sadness, a cry for forgiveness, entering into a confessional. All these things are in the Russian church, too. But to the Russian, repentance is a *bright sadness.*

When he begins to feel the grace of repentance, which is a gift from the Holy Spirit, he thanks God for the ability to be repentant, even though he isn't moving anywhere, yet. Then, he begins to cry. It comes spontaneously. He hasn't gone to confession. He's not thinking about going to confession, yet. He is in his sadness. Sin is sadness. It carries little guilt, but a lot of sadness. So he cries, "Oh, I have crucified God. I mean, my sins were part of his death." Then, after he has seen what he has done to God, he sits down and looks at God, and says, "But look, beyond Golgotha, there is Easter." And in the heart, hope springs up.

Repentance shot through with hope is fantastic and beautiful. You can almost dance. He who cried, dances towards the church to go to confession, because he has seen the bright side of sadness.

Now, with great joy, he goes to confession, because in his mind something has happened. He feels himself to be a child. At that moment of bright sadness, or repentance, he feels so totally a child that he says, "Ha, let me *run* to God. The lap of the Father is waiting. I'll jump into it, put my arms around his neck, and say to him, 'Father, I have sinned, but I love you.' What is God going to do? It's obvious. He is going to kiss me back." Lord, give me the heart of a child, and the awesome courage to live it out.

All this is connected by him with the Resurrection. We love confessions. We're not afraid of them. I think of confession as a joyful event. Something glorious. God has forgiven me. Alleluia! Alleluia! Alleluia! It is so exciting. I feel like going to confession again this minute.

The main thing to remember is that you are talking to God. Saying sorry to anybody is a beautiful thing, but to say I am sorry to God is especially beautiful. It makes you free, completely free. Try it sometime. Let that freedom enter your heart and go around saying to yourself, "Alleluia, alleluia, alleluia!"

To me, repentance is *making new*. With God, every moment is the moment of beginning again. Every time I repent over my sins, over my mistakes, over all these things, I renew myself in the sacrament of Penance. From the sacrament of Penance, I come as a newborn child out of the water of Baptism. I am renewed and full of grace. This is why I hope you will never feel guilty, because the amazing thing about God is that the guilt is washed out with every repentance. "If we acknowledge our sins, then God who is faithful and just will forgive our sins and cleanse us from everything that is wrong" (1 Jn 1:9).

Jesus began his preaching with this message: "Repent, for the kingdom of heaven is close at hand" (Mt 4:17). The key to the entry into the kingdom of heaven, which is within us, is repentance. We see it throughout the whole gospel, and it is so beautiful. People asked him to heal them, and he said, "Arise, your sins are forgiven you." "Your faith has made you whole" (Mt 9:5; Mk 2:5; 5:34; Lk 5:23; 7:48; 8:48). Faith and repentance have made you whole.

When I attend prayer meetings and people ask for healing, I ask for their repentance in my heart, because the healing will not take place until repentance takes place. I don't know if they have anything to repent for, but I think all of us have, so why not pray for repentance? They would rather pray for healing—same thing. Without one there is not the other.

Repentance is not a confession of past sins only. Repentance is a turning around. Some people think that if I sin, and then apologize and go to confession and get forgiven and all the rest of it, then I have repented. Repentance is much more than that. Repentance is really doing what I know I must do. Repentance is the incarnation of the gospel in a person's life. "The time has come, and the kingdom of God is close at hand. Repent, and believe the Good News" (Mk 1:15).

I have acknowledged that I have sinned before the Lord. I have acknowledged that I have trodden the wrong path. This I have done. But now I must turn my back to all of that and move in the *opposite* direction. Otherwise, in a little while, I will be telling the same story all over again to another priest or to the same priest.

To repent is to change. It is not just to acknowledge that I have done wrong. It is to turn my back to the wrong and start doing right, incarnating the gospel. The answer of Christianity to the world of today hinges on this. The world

Some/most change doesn't happen over night. it's a process.

of today believes that what Christ taught us doesn't have any value, because we do not incarnate it.

How are we going to incarnate the gospel? In a sense, it is awfully simple. We just have to stop personality clashes, judgment of one another, mistrust of one another, anger against one another, hostility against one another. We have to begin to love one another as Christ loved us. Then, the pagans of today will say, "Look at those Christians! They've really got something. See how they love one another."

Repentance is more than penitence, remorse, admitting mistakes. It is not saying in condemnation, "I've been a fool." Who of us has not recited such dismal litanies? All of us have. They are common and easy to recite. Repentance is more. It is even more than being sorry for one's sins. It is a moral and spiritual revolution. It calls for a complete breakdown of pride, of self-assurance, of prestige that comes from success, of the innermost citadel of self-will.

Unless we turn to God, we shall perish. God comes to us, tenderness, forgiveness, love, calling us to repentance, so that he might embrace us, so that he might bring us peace. What are we going to do? To repent is one of the hardest things in the world, yet it is basic to all spiritual progress.

Bathe Your Heart with Tears

St. Ambrose says of the two conversions that, in the Church, "there are water and tears: the water of Baptism and the tears of repentance" (Catechism of the Catholic Church, 1429).

Christ was once invited to some kind of dinner. A woman who was not exactly what she should be was there, a beautiful woman who was washing his feet with her tears and drying them with her beautiful hair. Throughout the room there was the scent of fragrant ointment that she was pouring on his feet.

"She waited behind him at his feet, weeping, and her tears fell on his feet, and she wiped them away with her hair; then she covered his feet with kisses and anointed them with the ointment" (Lk 7:38).

Whoever invited him for dinner was astonished that he allowed a prostitute, a woman with a bad name, to wash his feet and dry them with her hair. The people who had invited him, the big shots, the VIPs were thinking and whispering among themselves, "If this man were a prophet, he would know who this woman is that is touching him and what a bad name she has" (Lk 7:39).

The host had not done for Christ all the politeness and kindness that Jews extend to Jews when they invite each other to dinner. Jesus turned and said, "Do you see this woman? I entered your house, you gave me no water for my feet, but she has wet my feet with her tears and wiped them with her hair. You gave me no kiss, but from the time I came in she has not ceased to kiss my feet. You did not anoint my head with oil, but she has anointed my feet with ointment. Therefore I tell you, her sins, which are many, are forgiven, for she loved much" (Lk 7:44–47 RSV).

To me the judgment of Christ is mercy and tenderness and gentleness, and I have never had any fear of judgment, provided I say that I am sorry. I would tremble if I didn't say, "I am sorry."

Jesus turned around and spoke to the woman, "Your sins are forgiven." he told her, "Your faith has saved you; go in peace" (Lk 7:49–50).

You're a Saved Sinner

"For almighty God…because he is supremely good, would never allow any evil whatsoever to exist in his works if he were not so all-powerful and good as to cause good to emerge from evil itself" (St. Augustine, Catechism of the Catholic Church, *311*).

Baptism washes away our sin, but we can still sin any time. "The Lord…left man free to make his own decisions" (Eccl 15:14). God knows that after Baptism we will continue to sin, that we will be falling down flat on our face all the time. He knows we're sinful. So he has given us the sacrament of Penance.

We are all sinners. "Out of the depths I cry to you, O Lord. Behold my day. I haven't swept, I haven't dusted, I haven't tended to my children, I have double-crossed my husband, I have been taken in adultery. Behold me!" And a man is writing on the sand, "Woman, has anybody condemned you?" "No, sir." "Neither do I. Go and sin no more" (Jn 8:8–11). God loves sinners.

Yes, we are all sinners. But never forget that we are *saved* sinners. We are going to fall down a thousand times between birth and death; that is rather obvious. But immediately, we look at the gospel and see that God came for sinners, not for the perfect ones, if there be such. He said, "I did not come to call the virtuous, but sinners" (Mt 9:13). That means every one of us. Three cheers! You don't have to be perfect to be loved by God.

Yesterday, somebody was talking to me, and she said, "But I lack virtue. I am not up to par in fidelity. I am not good in this and in that." She really felt deeply that she wasn't worthy of God, because she wasn't full of all those virtues. But is that what God wants?

I said, "Have you ever considered that God loves sinners? And that we are all saved sinners?"

She said, "Yes, I know we are sinners, that is what bothers me."

I said, "That is what should cheer you up."

Christ came into the world to save sinners. The majority of people say yes to this with their lips but not with their hearts. They do not believe completely, totally, and without a single doubt that Christ came to this world to save sinners. They think that they should work hard so that God approves of them. They think that they are going to get to heaven on their own efforts, instead of remembering that Christ said, "Without me you can do nothing" (Jn 15:5 NAB). The result is a great tragedy.

Sure, we are sinners. We will fall down. But the arms of God are immense and embrace everybody. When you are guilty, say so to God through a confessor. Acknowledge your problems and sins. The moment you have stated them, God puts his hand over you, and you are a newborn babe. Cheer up, especially, you who are young and eternally worrying about the unnecessary things. Don't wallow in guilt. Wallow in the mercy of God. With God, every moment is the moment of beginning again.

A Forgiving Habit

It is not in our power not to feel or to forget an offense; but the heart that offers itself to the Holy Spirit turns injury into compassion and purifies the memory in transforming the hurt into intercession (Catechism of the Catholic Church, 2843).

Without forgiveness, which is the greatest sign of love, how can one receive the God of love? Jesus Christ himself prayed from the height of the cross, "Father, forgive them" (Lk 23:34).

There is something divine about forgiveness. Forgiveness is the fruit of love. The incredible, incomprehensible love of God is filled with forgiveness. Since we are baptized in the death and life of Jesus Christ, we should not allow the night to fall on our anger.

We should beg forgiveness and forgive every day. Forgiveness is not something you do just once or twice or twenty times, or a hundred times. It should grow into a virtue and become a habitual state.

Passionate love for mankind and pain: these two realities were like a chalice the Father had given Christ, and from which men would drink and know that he had forgiven them. This same chalice was also given to Mary, for in the incredible mystery of God's dealings with mankind, this woman was asked to share in the healing love, pain, and forgiveness that her son experienced on the cross.

Mary, the Mother of God, shared her divine son's passionate love for humanity, and she shared his pain. Her compassion bore the fruit of forgiveness. Her compassion and forgiveness bring healing to humanity. Because Mary accepted to share Christ's love, pain, and forgiveness, she became the Mother of us all, and people understand that they cannot walk through life without her, in a manner of speaking.

We are called to love one another. In order to love, one needs to forgive, and that means forgiving ourselves and everybody else. One cannot love the object of hostility, anger, hatred, and unforgiveness. Forgiveness is one of the urgent spiritual needs and actions. There is no use hiding behind rationalizations, no use sharpening our philosophical and theological arguments. Now is the time to forgive.

The Lord said, "Love your neighbor as yourself" (Mt 22:39), which means we must love ourselves first. We need to begin with forgiving ourselves as our Father in heaven forgives us. We may have gone to confession and been forgiven, but we remain uneasy, tragically feeling guilty of those very sins we have just confessed to God and have been absolved from. We do not really trust either his love or his forgiveness.

God does not want what has been forgiven to come back to haunt us or disturb us. Christ is always reconciling us to himself. We need to believe in his mercy and erasure.

On the human level, it is the same. When you have hurt somebody, have approached that person, and have been forgiven, then it is erased. It is over with, done with. The bond of love has been restored, and there is no memory of the tragic moment of unloosing that would stop you from loving further.

Simply, sincerely, and with grave humility we are to acknowledge our sins before ourselves. We go into the very depths of our souls and bring our faults out into the light. Then, after having begged forgiveness of them from God, we forgive ourselves.

Then, we go to the person, without any residual anger in some tiny corner of our heart, and really mean what we say when we apologize. While you are meditating on what you have done, come to a great and beautiful love—not a "liking"—a love for the one you have offended, a love that will grow in your heart so that barriers will fall down.

Forgiveness is a very deep thing. "I am sorry," is often said superficially. One needs to face the fact that one has wronged another person and go through a very great *kenosis* or emptying of self. In this situation, a person has to humiliate himself. Then, pure of heart and open to being humiliated by himself, he can approach the humble Christ in his brother or sister with a real and deep sorrow, not a superficial thing, and really look at the ways he has hurt the other.

What a beautiful thing it is to be reconciled with a brother or sister. When we are truly reconciled with one another, we can celebrate, with a celebration that is joyous and glad, full of laughter and song.

There is also the fantastic joy of the one who forgives. It's a spontaneous gesture, a gesture of open arms. As the other person begins his apology, already he is embraced, already a new ring is placed on his finger and new clothes on his back, as it says in the gospel of the return of the prodigal son (Lk 15:11–32). The father forgave, he ran forward, and so ought we. Whoever comes to us because they have done some hurt to us, if they apologize, we are called to act as did the father of the prodigal son, but even more, as Christ constantly does to us. Then, forgiveness becomes celebration.

Humility allows people to be open with one another, because the humble one has nothing to hide. Humility leads to openness. Let my life be known as it is, for whatever I have done or whatever I have been, I am a saved sinner. I have sinned many times, alas and alack, and I have this and that fault, but that is about the situation of everybody. So, why hide it? There's nothing to hide.

In the Russian tradition, we do not confuse humility and humiliation, for humility is truth. But we say that he who knows truth is open to humiliation, with joy. It's as if you're a doormat, and somebody with hobnailed boots walks over you, and you rejoice and kiss those feet with hobnailed boots. The ones who are really humble know how to be humiliated. The humiliated ones are the blessed of God, when they have accepted it.

It is true that forgiveness, mercy, and compassion may and probably will lead to that other truth uttered by Christ, "No one can have greater love than to lay down his life for his friends" (Jn 15:13). But wouldn't it be wonderful to die trying to forgive and love, rather than to die with hatred in one's heart?

Forgiveness can become a habitual state in which one forgives almost while one gets rejected, ignored, spat upon, or whatever. My forgiveness is given ahead of the deed, even as God grants it to all of us. There is about this forgiveness business something divine, closely aligned to charity, to love, and to God. When we really love God, we must activate that love by forgiving.

Face Your Enemies with Forgiveness

In refusing to forgive our brothers and sisters, our hearts are closed and their hardness makes them impervious to the Father's merciful love; but in confessing our sins, our hearts are opened to his grace (Catechism of the Catholic Church, 2844).

Something happens when I say, "I'm sorry." God's forgiveness is like a fire. It goes through me like a fire.

But his forgiveness won't go anywhere, it'll be returned, if I don't forgive my neighbor. Christ said, "When you stand in prayer, forgive whatever you have against anybody, so that your Father in heaven may forgive your failings too" (Mk 11:25). Now this is the big challenge of our lives. Whatever we have against anybody is hidden so deeply in our hearts that sometimes we even think that it belongs to the psychiatrist, but it doesn't. It belongs to the heart, not to the emotions.

I asked the Lord to help me understand better what the word *forgiveness* means. Forgiveness is so subtle, so beautiful, so perfect. When man forgives, he becomes like God. To forgive really is divine. Consider how many times God forgives us. In each of our lives, young or old, we have been forgiven by God one thousand million times, either when we simply said, "I'm sorry," or through confession. That is the amazing part about the forgiveness of God. There is just one little thing that we have to do—say two words: "I'm sorry." We commit sin, we say we are sorry, and he forgives us.

"Peter came up and said to him, 'Lord, how often shall my brother sin against me, and I forgive him? As many as seven times?' Jesus said to him, 'I do not say to you seven times, but seventy times seven'" (Mt 18:21–22). When the apostles asked Christ how many times they should forgive, he said, "Seventy times seven," which I understand from scripture scholars means *infinitely, without end.* So we are supposed to forgive our brother.

We, the unmerciful ones, the proud ones, we are supposed to forgive. The tragedy of many is that they can't forgive, though they know themselves to be forgiven by God. They usually have a scapegoat, and the scapegoat with married people is either the husband or the wife; with priests and religious, it is the superior or bishop. They didn't "understand" them; they didn't "do" this, that, and the other thing that they should have; they didn't give full recognition; and so on.

To forgive is to die to self. To forgive is to grow, grow until we can reach the toes of God. We have to accept people as they are and start from there. Otherwise, there is really no forgiveness, because God accepts me as I am, and he does not compel me to change. He invites me to change.

I keep asking people if they believe in God's commandment, "Love your enemies" (Mt 5:44). If your superior is your enemy, if your wife is impossible, if your husband cannot be trusted, then why don't you begin to believe in what God said? *Love your enemies.* Perhaps your love will change the face of that "enemy." If our forgiveness isn't accepted, we have to turn the other cheek. This is not easy, but Christ, who is the way, found the going pretty rough, too. So if we are walking within him, that is what we can expect also.

The more we forgive, the better we understand God's forgiveness. The more we trust each other, the better we understand God's trust. We should go to the same extent as God—trust the untrustworthy. Simply trust, and then hope will walk with us like a friend. Hope is musical. It has songs that you have never heard before. It is always a little ahead of you, dancing away with a song so that you can't help but follow it, if you have faith, love, trust, confidence in God.

If anybody knew about mercy, it was Paul. He was persecuting all the Christians. He was killing people. Then, God zapped him. Paul had been full of hatred. Later, when he was testifying for God, everybody deserted him. What does he say? Immediately, he says: may they not be held guilty. Remember that. It is a very good point for all of us to remember. Sometimes God offers us difficult choices. Paul forgave everybody, "The first time I had to present my defense, there was not a single witness to support me. Every one of them deserted me—may they not be held accountable for it" (2 Tm 4:16).

Is there really anything to forgive when you come right down to it? Look into your life. I can look into mine. Understand something. God uses other people as instruments to make us a little holier. *So we owe them a note of thanks.* Did you ever consider that?

My father used to say that obstacles are placed before you by God so that you might overcome them. Anything can become an obstacle. So just jump over it, he said, don't go around it. Well, he had a good point. He was a wise man. So ever since, I've tried to jump over obstacles. If there is anything to face, I'll say, "Okay, let's face it." Whenever you have an obstacle, face it directly, because in the business of Christianity, *if the truth is on your side, so is Christ.*

Meditate on forgiveness in depth. There is so much to it, because forgiveness comes from love. If you forgive, perhaps you will never need a psychiatrist. If you forgive your neighbor, you will experience the healing of all the memories which need healing.

Let us enlarge the circle of love in our heart, so that it can encompass humanity, the humanity that flows around, through, and by us. Such love is the love of God. Forgiveness is part of it. Humility sings a song to it. Mercy flows from it. Let us join hands in deep forgiveness of one another. Let us reconcile ourselves to anyone with whom we are not yet reconciled. Let us forget any attachment to anything that isn't God.

O Jesus,
how far from fulfilling your precepts I am!
Look at me,
after years of your love, your grace, your help,
I'm still the same proud, sinful, erring, slothful,
    sensual person.
It seems I have not started on the right road,
    even now.
Yet whatever my faults,
I shall never doubt your mercy.
On it, I throw myself.
In it, I hide, for in it alone lies my salvation.
I believe and trust in you with all my faculties.
O Jesus, have mercy on me a sinner.
I will never remain lying in the mire,
no matter how deeply I fall.
I shall get up at once,
and, trusting and repentant,
start again and again,
for in you alone is life.
Amen.

Chapter Six

Reconciliation

It is the Lord who speaks—
"Come back to me with all your heart,
fasting, weeping, mourning."
Let your hearts be broken, not your garments torn,
turn to the Lord your God again,
for he is all tenderness and compassion,
slow to anger, rich in graciousness,
and ready to relent.

Joel 2:12–13

How Do You Love

"The commandments: 'You shall not commit adultery, You shall not kill, You shall not steal, You shall not covet,' and any other commandment, are summed up in this sentence: 'You shall love your neighbor as yourself.' Love does no wrong to a neighbor; therefore love is the fulfilling of the law" (Romans 13:9–10, Catechism of the Catholic Church, 2055).

When I was a girl, the Russian people did not have confessionals. The priest sat under an icon in front of everybody, and you came to him and knelt down and told him your sins. Usually, his first question was "How do you love your enemies?"

When I was ten or so, I couldn't think of any enemies, and he said, "You love all the girls in your class?"

I immediately remembered six that I disliked intensely, so he worked on me and changed this. I started loving them. I don't know how.

Then, the priest asked how you love your neighbor.

That is about the end of the conversation, because if you love, you are not going to fornicate, you are not going to commit adultery, you are not going to be avaricious. You are not going to do any of the things that are the seven deadly sins, because they are all against charity.

Why don't we all think today of the second commandment: "Love your neighbor as yourself" (Mt 22:39). The first neighbor that you and I have is ourselves. The first neighbor that you have is yourself and that I have is myself. I am supposed to love myself in the right way, for I am created in the image and likeness of God.

It is strange not to love myself when God loves me. Concentrate on what Christ said. Maybe he will help us to love ourselves in such a manner that we are able to love others. I can't love others until I come to love myself.

You Affect Everyone's Friendship with God

"If you are the body and members of Christ, then it is your sacrament that is placed on the table of the Lord; it is your sacrament that you receive. To that which you are, you respond 'Amen' ('yes, it is true!') and by responding to it you assent to it. For you hear the words, 'the Body of Christ' and respond 'Amen.' Be then a member of the Body of Christ that your Amen may be true" (St. Augustine, Catechism of the Catholic Church, 1396).

When I commit a sin, you all suffer. If you commit a sin, we all suffer. Because of that, I think all sins are tragic. Sin affects the whole Body of Christ.

The East does not worry about sins juridically. The East weeps over its sins, because they are offenses against charity, against love for God and one's fellowmen. When I commit a sin, even if it's alone in my apartment or hidden in the dark recesses of my soul, I sin against the whole Body of Christ, against all the people of God. No matter how hidden my sin, it affects the whole mystical Body of Christ.

I'm a nurse. If I am taking care of a patient and get a little pinprick from his splinter, I feel pain the next day. If I don't take care of it, I may develop an infection from some germ that will spread. I may die. Sin is like that pinprick. What I do affects everybody. My sin reverberates across the rest of the world.

Sin makes God sad, and his Church sad, too; after all, *you* are his Church, *we* are the people of God. "The gathering together of the People of God began at the moment when sin destroyed the communion of men with God, and that of men among themselves. The gathering together of the Church is, as it were, God's reaction to the chaos provoked by sin" (*Catechism*, 761).

It is in Christ that the brotherhood of man is established. He's the brother of man. Christ died for Buddhists, atheists, Moslems, Christians, and everybody. "Reunification is achieved secretly in the heart of all peoples." Faith is a mystery, a gift of God that joins us in the brotherhood of Christ. "God does not have favorites...anybody of any nationality who fears him and does what is right is acceptable to him" (*Catechism*, 761, Acts 10:35). Ultimately, all things come together in the apex of Christ, the whole cosmos comes together.

But Christ died so that we may repent and be forgiven. "Wishing to open up the way to heavenly salvation, [God] manifested himself to our first parents from the very beginning. He invited them to intimate communion with himself and clothed them with resplendent grace and justice. This revelation was not broken off by our first parents' sin. After the fall, [God] buoyed them up with the hope of salvation, by promising redemption; and he has never ceased to show his solicitude for the human race. For he wishes to give eternal life to all those who seek salvation by patience in well-doing" (*Catechism*, 54–55). Christ is in our midst. Christ has risen from the dead. He comes to us with tenderness, forgiveness, love, calling us to repentance, so that he might embrace us, so that he might bring us peace.

"After the unity of the human race was shattered by sin God at once sought to save humanity part by part" (*Catechism*, 56). "Sin damages or even breaks fraternal communion. The sacrament of Penance repairs or restores it. In this sense, it does not simply heal the one restored to ecclesial communion, but has also a revitalizing effect on the life of the Church which suffered from the sin of one of her members. Re-established or strengthened in the communion of saints, the sinner is made stronger by the exchange of spiritual goods among all the living members of the Body of Christ, whether still on pilgrimage or already in the heavenly homeland" (*Catechism*, 1469).

Our lack of reconciliation, forgiveness, and thoughtfulness is at the bottom of the world's mess. We haven't got them, and the world is in a mess. "Man and sinner are, so to speak, two realities: when you hear 'man'—this is what God has made; when you hear 'sinner'—this is what man himself has made. Destroy what you have made, so that God may save what he has made" (St. Augustine, *Catechism* 1458). Do we, as Christians, as people who believe in God, show the face of Christ on the streets of our cities? The state of the world depends on us.

"The Church, in Christ, is like a sacrament—a sign and instrument, that is, of communion with God and of unity among all men. The Church's first purpose is to be the sacrament of the *inner union of men with God.* Because men's communion with one another is rooted in that union with God, the Church is also the sacrament of the *unity of the human race.* In her, this unity is already begun, since she gathers men from every nation, from all tribes and peoples and tongues; at the same time, the Church is the 'sign and instrument' of the full realization of the unity yet to come" (*Catechism*, 775).

Leadership in love must come from those who profess to be followers of Christ, of the God of Abraham, of the Lord. Yes, let us cry the gospel with our lives and the whole world will enter into its springtime, and the storms will be hushed, and peace will reign among us.

"As sacrament, the Church is Christ's instrument. She is taken up by him also as the instrument for the salvation of all, the universal sacrament of salvation, by which Christ is at once manifesting and actualizing the mystery of God's love for men. The Church is the visible plan of God's love for humanity, because God desires that the whole human race may become one People of God, form one Body of Christ, and be built up into one temple of the Holy Spirit" (*Catechism*, 776).

It starts with me, changing my style of life, changing my heart. We need a change of heart even more than a change of lifestyle. I'm so deeply united with all the rest of mankind that what I do and what I don't do affects the whole world.

Love Begins with You

"Come, Holy Spirit, fill the hearts of your faithful and enkindle in them the fire of your love" (Catechism of the Catholic Church, 2671).

Christ seeks himself in every heart. Will he find himself in my heart?

The beginning is ourselves, each one of us. We are the unknown lands. Begin at the beginning. Christ said, "Love your neighbor as yourself." Who is this self that God wants us to love first, before we try to love anyone else? Would I take a bus, train, or plane to discover my own utter poverty, my own need of God?

We are the poorest of the poor. "Love your neighbor *as yourself.*" Unless we truly love ourselves, we cannot even begin to love our neighbors. I may adore Christ in *their* hearts, but such adoration will be sterile and empty—it is a useless journey, unless I see the image of God in my own heart.

The Lord wants us to grow in faith and love of him, trusting in him alone. Without faith, we cannot see the image of God in our own hearts, we cannot love ourselves. If we see him in ourselves, then we will be able to see him in others. Then, the Christ in us can meet the Christ in the other.

"Reconciliation with God leads, as it were, to other reconciliations, which repair the other breaches caused by sin. The forgiven penitent is reconciled with himself in his inmost being, where he regains his innermost truth. He is reconciled with his brethren whom he has in some way offended and wounded. He is reconciled with the Church. He is reconciled with all creation" (John Paul II, *Catechism*, 1469). Having been scooped up by the hand of God, and having agreed to it by your yes, you become a transparent bonfire that leads other men to Christ.

God allows men to be tempted so that they may grow in faith, love, and hope. In the Eastern tradition, temptations are seen as stepping stones. God is calling you to come up higher, and Christ, your brother, is saying to you, "I am here, and I have conquered evil and death on the Cross. So give me your hand and the Evil One will be but a stepping-stone to where you wish to go." The Lord, from time immemorial, has known you. His fire is over you.

"Creation has its own goodness and proper perfection, but it did not spring forth complete from the hands of the Creator. The universe was created 'in a state of journeying' (*in statu viae*) toward an ultimate perfection yet to be attained, to which God has destined it. We call 'divine providence' the dispositions by which God guides his creation toward this perfection" (*Catechism*, 302). You are moving slowly up his mountain. To get to the top you must pass through the heart of God.

Self-knowledge is one of the greatest graces that God can give us. "When man looks into his own heart he finds that he is drawn towards what is wrong and sunk in many evils which cannot come from his good creator. Often refusing to acknowledge God as his source, man has also upset the relationship which should link him to his last end, and at the same time he has broken the right order that should reign within himself as well as between himself and other men and all creatures" (*Catechism*, 401).

No one wants to face his emotional self. Nobody wants to admit that he or she acts at times like a 10-year-old, that they have a thousand different moods, that they are afraid of the silliest things. We are beginning to know who we are, our difficulties, our sins, seeing with more clarity of soul. Stand still, don't run away. Flight from oneself into feverish activity is often a flight, an escape from meeting oneself. Stand still. Such is what writers in Eastern spirituality offer as a remedy against the temptations of the devil.

You will be tempted. "The new life received in Christian initiation has not abolished the frailty and weakness of human nature, nor the inclination to sin…which remains in the baptized such that with the help of the grace of Christ they may prove themselves in the struggle of Christian life." "Man is divided in himself. As a result, the whole life of men, both individual and social, shows itself to be a struggle, and a dramatic one, between good and evil, between light and darkness" (*Catechism*, 1426, 1707).

How do you overcome evil? By the sign of the cross, the invocation of the name of Jesus and of Our Lady, and, above all, by faith. If you are afraid, talk with your spiritual director. (A confessor specifically deals with confessional matters during a confession. A spiritual director usually sees the directee in a manner impossible for the short time allotted to a confession, though, the director might hear a confession to direct a soul better toward sanctity.) Lean more on God, and reach out to him like a drowning man reaches out to a floating log. In the knowledge that without God we can do nothing, we reach a high point of understanding. When we experience in the darkness, in the fear, in the terror, in the panic that his grace is indeed sufficient for us, this becomes the moment of real believing. We come to see that if God has permitted the tempter to come to us, then God will give us the grace to resist him.

Russians believe that the greatest purity is achieved through tears, tears that really wash us. These are never tears of anger, or tears of animosity toward anyone. Our tears mingle with the tears of Christ and cleanse the soul of every extraneous thing that is bothering it. Tears wash away every interior attachment that hinders true poverty of spirit. Tears are also another way through which we come to appreciate the great gift of God—our freedom. Our soul, washed by tears, can see clearly that we really are free, that we can say yes or no to God.

The clarity achieved by these tears does not mean that now the soul is sinless, nor does it mean that we are saints. It just means that my soul has been cleansed by God, that I have been able to recognize who I am—with all my arrogance, my pride, my self-will. But we have reached some new level where we can recognize that the arrogance is there, and the recognition leads us closer to God. This is clarity of soul. Reconcile with God. Then, forgive yourself; reconcile with yourself. Then, reconcile yourself with the other and the whole world. A new light will rise in you, God's light. "Indeed the sacrament of Reconciliation with God brings about a true 'spiritual resurrection,' restoration of the dignity and blessings of the life of the children of God, of which the most precious is friendship with God" (*Catechism*, 1468).

Reconcile with Yourself

Forgiveness is the fundamental condition of the reconciliation of the children of God with their Father and of men and with one another (Catechism of the Catholic Church, 2844).

Last night I was thinking of reconciliation and wondering what makes reconciliation possible among people. Forgiveness. Forgiveness makes reconciliation possible.

In a flash, I realized that forgiveness will bring reconciliation, and I knew then that it had to be among nations, among peoples, and among us.

We have to be reconciled first to God, then to ourselves, and then to the whole world and to whomever hurt us.

It is *God* who has reconciled us, and it is through Jesus Christ that he has done so. "Be reconciled to God. For our sake God made the sinless one into sin, so that in him we might become the goodness of God" (2 Cor 5:20–21). Jesus, obedient unto death, death on a cross, took our sins upon himself. Only thus could we be reconciled to God.

And now, because Christ has done so, *we also* have the gift of reconciliation, that is to say, we can reconcile ourselves with our brethren. "It is all God's work. It was God who reconciled us to himself through Christ and gave us the work of handing on this reconciliation" (2 Cor 5:18). "We are ambassadors for Christ; it is as though God were appealing through us, and the appeal that we make in Christ's name is: be reconciled to God" (2 Cor 5:20). We have the power to become ambassadors of God, of forgiveness and reconciliation.

Just as God has dealt with us through Jesus Christ, we now must deal with others. To strive for this surrender to him, this reconciliation with our brothers and sisters in him, is to tear out by the roots the shrubs of one's own will and put them into a fire that consumes. "As his fellow workers, we beg you once again not to neglect the grace of God that you have received" (2 Cor 6:1).

People who don't do the will of God are the unhappiest, most miserable human beings on earth. "We all want to live happily; in the whole human race there is no one who does not assent to this proposition, even before it is fully articulated" (St. Augustine, *Catechism*, 1718). "This desire is of divine origin: God has placed it in the human heart in order to draw man to the One who alone can fulfill it" (*Catechism*, 1718). Sometimes they know their unhappiness is caused by not doing God's will, and sometimes they don't. Of course, if they don't know it, then we have to pray for them, but if they know, then something has to be done to achieve reconciliation.

As I prayed, it came to me that I have to forgive myself. Forgiveness comes from love. So you must love *yourself* first. We have to begin to love ourselves as Christ said, "Love your neighbor as yourself" (Mt 22:39)—*as yourself*. What have we got to forgive ourselves for? Well, mostly for the fact that we haven't done the will of God. First, you have to reconcile yourself with yourself. Then, you can go on to reconciling yourself with the other.

Forgiveness is generosity, tenderness, understanding, and deep healing. If you forgive your neighbor, you will experience the healing of memories that need healing. The healing of memories means forgiveness. Forgiveness to the society we came from that might have hurt our psyches. Forgiveness for the pain that we may have experienced and didn't even know it while we were in our mothers' wombs. Forgiveness to mothers. Forgiveness to parents who have misunderstood us, neglected us, rejected us, and so on.

From there on, like lightning going through a darkened sky, our forgiveness will cover itself and scan like the light of a lighthouse scans the sea. Whenever that light sees anything that we think hurts us, the touch of the light will bring forgiveness into our heart and bless the person we forgive.

But we have to do more. After having forgiven, if our forgiveness wasn't accepted, if our reconciliation was thrown back at us, we have to turn the other cheek. That is what is meant by the two beatitudes of the Lord: "Happy the lowly, they shall have the earth for their heritage," and "Happy are you when people abuse you and persecute you and speak all kinds of calumny against you on my account. Rejoice and be glad, for your reward will be great in heaven" (Mt 5:4, 11–12). If we implement them, we will be meek, and the meek shall inherit the earth, as well as heaven.

"We have been given possession of an unshakable kingdom. Let us therefore hold on to the grace that we have been given and use it to worship God in the way that he finds acceptable.... Our God is a consuming fire" (Heb 12:28–29). "From now onward, therefore, we do not judge anyone by the standards of the flesh. And for anyone who is in Christ, there is a new creation; the old creation has gone, and now the new one is here. It's all God's work" (2 Cor 5:16–18). Let us be consumed with God, and we will change the face of the earth.

Make Peace

Forgiveness bears witness that, in our world, love is stronger than sin (Catechism of the Catholic Church, 2844).

I have to look around and say, "With whom should I be reconciled?" I should be reconciled with the whole world and with the people that are close to me.

It might be a checkout clerk. Say you went to a store and pushed your cart through her lane, and you were impolite to her because she was going in slow motion. You should go back, apologize, and reconcile yourself. There might be a taxi driver that you bawled out. If you can find him again, if he is near your place, go and reconcile yourself. It is not only your friends that you should be reconciled with, but also the ordinary people that pass your way again and again and again.

Sometimes during Mass, we pray the *Confiteor* so perfunctorily:

"I confess to almighty God and to you, my brothers and sisters, that I have sinned through my own fault, in my thoughts and in my words, in what I have done and in what I have failed to do, and I ask blessed Mary, ever virgin, and all the angels and saints, and you, my brothers and sisters, to pray for me to the Lord our God." Suppose we stopped there and really turned to someone.

If I feel mad at someone, then I have to get out of my little corner, bow before her and say, "Sorry I was mad at you. Forgive me." It would do us a lot of good if we tried to do that. Christ said, "If your brother has something against you, leave your gifts at the altar, and go and make peace with your brother" (Mt 5:23–24). One of the reasons why we don't do it is because we are afraid of each other. There is always that horrible fear. Fear of being different. Fear of ridicule. Fear of your age group. There are thousands of fears that come forth and hold us back from God and keep us from opening the door to freedom. Once we get rid of that fear, we are free.

Go to your brother or sister. It might not come off at all. Maybe it will get worse, or people will call you names and throw you out. That happens, too. We resent it when people don't come through the way we expect them to.

Remember, Christ said that blessed are you who are persecuted for his name's sake, you will get your reward in heaven (Mt 5:11–12). That is what happens when you go to a person to tell him you are sorry, and he throws you out. But you have made it with God. Never mind the person.

You have to reconcile yourself as you walk along the road of life. Even better than reconciliation is thoughtfulness. I said to myself yesterday, the trouble with us is that we are *thoughtless*. Not that we are selfish, not that we are anything like that, we just are without thought. We move, we act, we do things without thought, and we hurt people. We leave misunderstanding. We leave doubt. We leave mistrust. We leave tragedy. That sort of thing must not happen. We must be *thought-full*, because we are Christians. A Christian is one who is always thinking about the other. God first, my neighbor second, myself last. When we get to that stage, reconciliation is as easy as falling off a log.

Forgiveness comes naturally. In fact, we can't sleep if we don't go and apologize to other people or reconcile ourselves to other people.

Anything that comes between my neighbor and me divides nations like a cellophane sheet. We can glare at each other without touching each other. It all begins with me. It is because of me that people are tortured, that people are fleeing their countries. It is because I am not what I should be that all the tragedies of the world happen.

Hold Me Tight

"I did not create you to be a prisoner in hell" (*Ancient Homily for Holy Saturday,* Catechism of the Catholic Church, 635).

St. Paul says, "God has reconciled us to himself through Christ, and given us the ministry of reconciliation" (2 Cor 5:18). This is a fantastic word. You could almost take it out of context and its sound alone is healing: *reconciliation.* To be reconciled with another. It means forgiving and being forgiven. It means an opening to love on both sides. It really means healing. It is a tremendous word.

We must change our hearts, enlarge them, and allow God to come in, be reconciled with him. What do I mean, "be reconciled with him"? You know the commandments: love God, love your neighbor as yourself, love your enemies, lay down your life for your brethren. These are the laws of love, and these are the ones we have to follow. Unless we follow them we are not reconciled with ourselves, with our neighbor, or with God.

There is a restlessness about us. There are emotional sicknesses that shake us. Because we are not what we should be, the rest of the world is not what it should be, for the fate of the world rests in my sinful hands. If each of us were what we profess to be—Catholics, Protestants, Jews, or whatever—we would change the world.

We have to come back to reconciliation. Nobody can kiss me unless I want to be kissed. Do we want to be kissed by God? Do we want to be reconciled with him? Do we really want to obey his commandment of love? The word *obey* is silly in the sense that there is no yoke of obedience. He who loves obeys because he loves.

Will we really be reconciled at Mass? Will we really shed all that junk that fills our minds and hearts and simply say, "Here I am, Lord, such as I am. I am sorry for anything wrong I have done, but I said I was sorry yesterday. I do want to be reconciled with you, because only in accepting the forgiveness of the Father in you will I restore this world to you. There is no other way that I can restore it. As long as I think I can do it on my own, the world will be filled with chaos."

The sacrament of confession is the sacrament of Reconciliation. The sacrament of confession suddenly takes on a tremendous power. It is not just something that one does automatically, or by rote, or because my father or mother taught me. Confession becomes a gift of God all over again.

God comes. God wants to kiss us, embrace us, hold us, like the father when he ran toward the prodigal. Are we ready for the embrace of God?

Confession becomes a cry in the night. There in the quiet night, God descends in Jesus Christ, and suddenly, from all over the world, we walk toward Bethlehem, almost lifted up, crying out in the night:

"Here I am. I want you to embrace me. Hold me tight, so that I never stray from you."

Lord of Mercy, bring us to our knees.
Give us the grace to weep over our sins.
Let the cocks of our consciences crow loudly thrice
to remind us that you alone
possess the answers to our anguish,
that you alone
can change darkness into light, sorrow into joy,
        death into life.

Lord of Love, open our dried-up little hearts.
Make them big—
big enough for you to come and dwell again
        therein.
Unveil our souls
that have enclosed themselves

in the dark fortresses of ourselves.
Set them free,
that they may destroy this idol, this self,
and adore again only you, the Adorable.

Lord of Light, be a lamp to our straying feet.
Set them on your path of love and joy.
Teach them to walk once more
in charity and self-forgetfulness.

Mary, Mother of God, bend down to us,
and turn our eyes upward and inward
so that we may be rid of our blindness,
and behold him

who came down from heaven through you,
to give us sight.
Be our star. Lead us back home.
Amen.

Sources

Writings and recordings of Catherine Doherty used in the preparation of this book are listed here. Unless otherwise noted, all books in italics are published by Madonna House Publications, Combermere, ON. Other items (those not in italics) are internal documents of the Madonna House Apostolate, Combermere, ON.

Chapter I: Healing

Audio recordings, masters no. 1206, 1712, 2512. Transcripts.

Dear Father: A Message of Love for Priests, 2001.

Dearly Beloved: Letters to the Children of My Spirit. Vols. I & III, 1989.

Diary. 24 January 1938.

Faith, 1997.

Letters from the Poustinia, no. 4.

Local Directors Meeting, 6 September 1979. Transcript.

Season of Mercy: Lent and Easter, 1996.

Staff Letters, no. 118.

Staff Letters from the Foundress, no. 54.

Welcome, Pilgrim, 1991.

Chapter II: Conversion

Where Love Is, God Is. Milwaukee: Bruce Publishing Co., 1953.

Diary. 28 May 1934, 24 September 1938.

Dear Seminarian: Letters from a Lay Apostle on Becoming a Shepherd of Souls, 2003.

Staff Letters from the Foundress, no. 111.

Season of Mercy.

Chapter III: Penance

Audio recordings, masters no. 1138, 2604. Transcripts.

Dear Parents: A Gift of Love for Families, 1997.

Diary. 28 March 1935, 20 August 1935.

Letters from the Poustinia, no. 30.

Living the Gospel Without Compromise, 2002.

Friendship House Outer Circle Letters, no. 135.

Season of Mercy.

Staff Letters, no. 29, 112, 116, 187, 189, 227.

To Follow Christ: Letters of Catherine Doherty to a Daughter in the Spirit, 1998.

Where Love Is, God Is.

Chapter IV: Confession

Audio recording, master no. 863. Transcript.

An Experience of God: Identification with Christ—a Road to the Mystical Life, 2002.

Bogoroditza: She Who Gave Birth to God, 1998.

Diary. 14 March 1936, 17 April 1936.

Faith.

Gospel of a Poor Woman, The, 1992.

Letters between Catherine Doherty and Father Paul Furfey, 21 March 1938, 9 May 1940, 24 July 1946.

Living the Gospel Without Compromise.

My Russian Yesterdays, 1990.

Friendship House Outer Circle Letters, no. 2, 7.

Staff Letters from the Foundress, no. 60.

Where Love Is, God Is.

Chapter V: Forgiveness

Dearly Beloved, Vol. III.

Diary. 13 January 1935.

Living the Gospel Without Compromise.

Poustinia: Encountering God in Silence, Solitude and Prayer, 2000.

Season of Mercy.

Staff Letters from the Foundress, no. 59, 84.

Chapter VI: Reconciliation

Gospel Without Compromise, The, 1989.

History of the Apostolate of Friendship House and Madonna House.

Letters from the Poustinia, no. 22.

Living the Gospel Without Compromise.

Poustinia.

Sobornost: Experiencing Unity of Mind, Heart and Soul, 2000.

Where Love Is, God Is.

About the Author

Born to wealthy parents in Russia in 1896, Catherine became a refugee in Canada during the Bolshevik revolution and experienced harsh poverty. Eventually recognized as a gifted lecturer, she became wealthy again, only to be pursued by the call of Christ to renounce everything to follow him.

Catherine intended to live a life of prayer and simple service to the poor in the slums but her example of radical Gospel living became a magnet for men and women in search of a way to live their faith. She founded Friendship Houses in Toronto and Harlem, and then the Madonna House community, based in Combermere, Ontario, where her formation of lay apostles extended to countless persons, and in a ceaselessly flowing river of articles, letters and books, she penetrated the lives of Christians, calling all to live the Gospel.

Catherine died in 1985 and her Cause for Canonization is in process; she is officially a 'Servant of God'.

Internet: www.catherinedoherty.org

Madonna House Publications
2888 Dafoe Rd, RR 2
Combermere ON   K0J 1L0
Canada

Internet: www.madonnahouse.org/publications

E-mail: publications@madonnahouse.org

Telephone: (613) 756-3728